NATURECRAFTS

50 Extraordinary Gifts and Projects, Step by Step

Gillian Souter

CROWN TRADE PAPERBACKS

New York

Published by Crown Trade Paperbacks, 201 East 50th Street, New York, New York 10022. Member of the Crown Publishing Group.

Random House, Inc. New York, Toronto, London, Sydney, Auckland

CROWN TRADE PAPBERBACKS and colophon are trademarks of Crown Publishers, Inc.

Originally published in Australia by Off the Shelf Publishing in 1996.

Printed in Hong Kong

LIBRARY OF CONGRESS CATALOGING-IN-PUBLICATION DATA
is available upon request.

ISBN 0-517-88533-6

10 9 8 7 6 5 4 3 2 1

First American Edition

Foreword

There is something especially fitting about the two words "nature" and "craft"; they sound right together. It is, after all, in human nature to fashion objects, either for decoration or for use in some way. In turn, nature offers us a diversity of raw materials to do so, with an abundance of shapes, colors, and textures. Step out of the city and, whether you're in a field, by the sea, or in a forest, you will be surrounded by materials which can be crafted into something even more pleasing.

This book touches on each type of material—leaves, shells, stones—and suggests some ways of bringing out their qualities. There are recurring ideas and techniques, such as plaiting and dyeing, which have been used for centuries and by different cultures. There are various methods made possible with modern equipment; there are some advantages to living in the age of hot glue guns and electric drills. Each chapter contains three projects:

 A personal item, ideal as a gift

Something useful for the home

 Items for special occasions

There are also tips on celebrating with the seasons and on using natural objects for gift wrapping and making greeting cards. Bring a bit of nature into the home and share it with friends and family when you turn your hand to nature crafts.

Contents

Collecting

One of the greatest problems you will face when looking for materials is what not to collect. Nature is full of interesting objects and it is tempting to squirrel them all away for possible use. Try to be selective: once you have a good example of a certain shell, let the others be. Take only enough pine cones for the project you have in mind. Leave some of those pebbles in the riverbed. This way, there will be something left for your child to collect in years to come.

This, of course, only applies to resources that aren't easily renewed and to environments which are precariously balanced, some of which will also be protected by law. If you can cultivate flowers, herbs, or fruit in your garden then there's no stopping you! Many of the items you might buy will be sold in bulk. Share an excess of such materials with your friends; something you value little might be a windfall for them.

When you have gathered bits and pieces, clean them and store them carefully. Few things are more frustrating than finding your treasure trove broken, covered with mildew, or depleted by insects. Label any containers of small objects and add the date of collection if they have a limited lifespan.

The best way to enjoy natural things is by putting them on display. Many of the projects in this book are concerned with showing things off—the sampler in Project 16, the collector's box in Project 51—but there are also many simpler ways of presenting such items. Put a few unusual pebbles around the base of a pot plant, or some shells in the bottom of a clear vase of flowers for extra interest. Heap spiky seedpods on a platter and set it at the center of the dinner table. Look to nature for some fresh ideas!

Anything pressed flat can be displayed in a glass paperweight which can be bought with a recessed back. Solid objects can be embedded in acrylic resin.

Objects which are naturally found in water, such as shells and tumbled stones, often have stronger colors when placed in a water-filled bowl or specimen vase such as this one.

A sampler is an excellent way to show off the variations and similarities between natural objects.

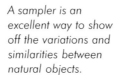

Arranged in an attractive bowl, with the less interesting samples underneath, a few well-selected pieces can look like a rich harvest.

Equipment

Most of the utensils required for the projects will be found in your kitchen cupboards or in the top drawer of your desk. Any items you don't have can usually be purchased from suppliers of craft materials or from large hardware stores.

Some useful equipment is available from florists' suppliers. Strong scissors or florist's snips are necessary for cutting thick stems and wires. Stub wires in pre-cut lengths are used to wire cones and bundles of fruit or foliage. Choose a suitable thickness for the particular task. Alternatively, you can cut your own pieces from a reel of thin wire. Stem tape, a flexible green tape, is handy for binding wires and for concealing them.

Various types of glue are recommended at different times. White craft glue is generally used, but a hot glue gun is ideal for fixing things in place quickly and spray adhesive is suitable for other situations. A craft knife and cutting mat will prove useful in many of the projects and are worthwhile investments.

Equipment and materials needed for each project are listed in a box above the project picture. If you don't have a specified item, read the instructions and you may find that an alternative utensil will do the same job just as well.

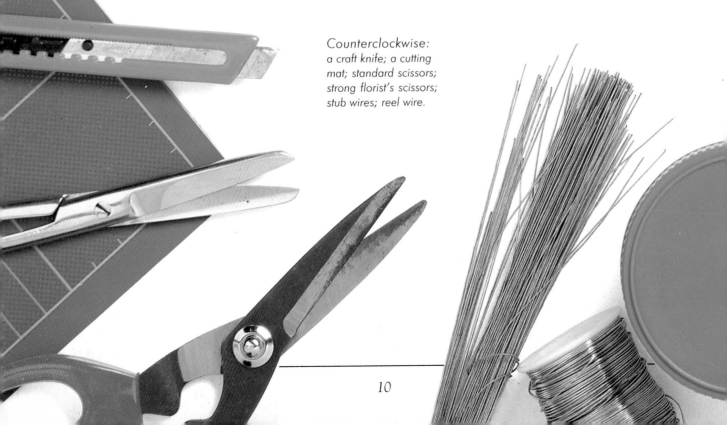

Counterclockwise:
a craft knife; a cutting
mat; standard scissors;
strong florist's scissors;
stub wires; reel wire.

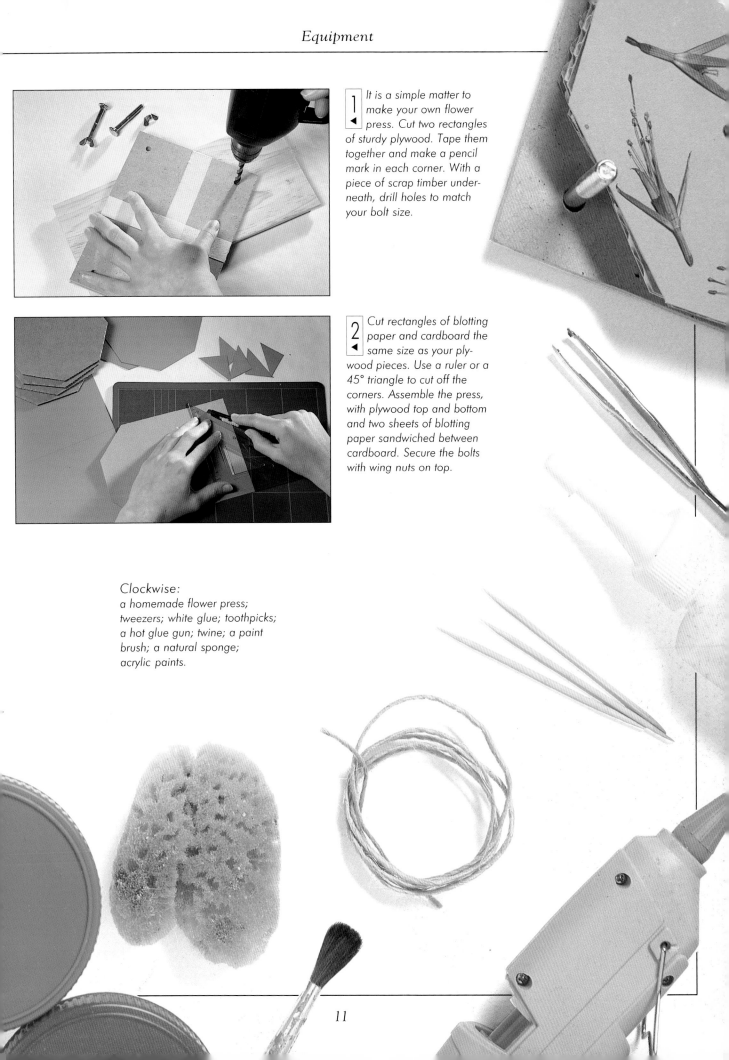

1 It is a simple matter to make your own flower press. Cut two rectangles of sturdy plywood. Tape them together and make a pencil mark in each corner. With a piece of scrap timber underneath, drill holes to match your bolt size.

2 Cut rectangles of blotting paper and cardboard the same size as your plywood pieces. Use a ruler or a 45° triangle to cut off the corners. Assemble the press, with plywood top and bottom and two sheets of blotting paper sandwiched between cardboard. Secure the bolts with wing nuts on top.

Clockwise:
a homemade flower press;
tweezers; white glue; toothpicks;
a hot glue gun; twine; a paint
brush; a natural sponge;
acrylic paints.

Basic Techniques

There are no mysteries to the techniques used in this book. Most of them will probably bring back memories of your first years at school, although you will now be allowed to use the scissors with sharp points! Many of the most simple procedures are also quite therapeutic: an hour spent braiding raffia can be surprizingly satisfying.

Techniques which apply to specific fibers or materials are discussed in the opening pages of each chapter and it is worthwhile reading through that text before undertaking relevant projects. These projects offer a starting point and will hopefully launch you into a further exploration of particular crafts which catch your interest.

Using Natural Colors

Colors in nature are seldom dull, but pale materials—sand, raffia, cane, hen's eggs—can be dyed to a different color to great effect. A wide range of hues can be achieved using chemical dyes but a natural alternative, and an important one when young children are crafting or if you want the project to be edible, is a non-toxic vegetable dye.

Onion skins, nutshells, and many herbs offer up a dye when boiled, while hot water added to ground coffee, tea, turmeric, or paprika will produce interesting coloring agents. The addition of salt and vinegar will help to fix the color. Other natural pigments can be made by grinding some charcoal or ocher which, with a little water added, makes a satisfactory paint.

If you plan to dye fabrics, it is necessary to treat them first by soaking them in a solution of alum and cream of tartar or other chemical mordants.

Braiding Fibers

Braiding is a method of interweaving long strips, whether of raffia, hessian, rush, or straw. The most common examples are long bands such as those shown here, but the technique can also be used to make flat surfaces and three-dimensional shapes. Below are instructions for braiding with a different number of strands. Choose the type most fitting for the purpose: a three-strand braid, shown on the immediate right, is the easiest to make and tends to be heavier and stronger than the other two. A five-strand braid, shown on the far right, requires some practice but is wider and so suitable for larger projects. People who are left-handed may prefer to work by reversing the diagram in a mirror.

Three-strand braid
Take strand 1, from the right, and cross it over 2, then cross 3 over the central strand and so on.

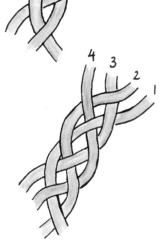

Four-strand braid
Take strand 1, from the right, and cross it under 2, over 3, then fold 4 over 1.

Five-strand braid
Take strand 1, from the right, and weave it over 2, under 3, over 4 and then fold 5 over 1.

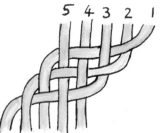

Papermaking

When you buy paper in reams or in rolls, it is easy to forget that paper is essentially a layer of intertwined plant fibers. The best way of reminding yourself is to make your own paper. Any material containing cellulose fiber can be used for making paper at home, as long as it can be broken down. Waste paper which has not been heavily inked can be soaked overnight and then pulped in a blender or liquidizer. Plant matter, such as celery, rhubarb, and corn husks, must be boiled for a long time and beaten to break them down.

You can make paper rounds by collecting the pulp in a sieve, but to make sheets of paper, you will need a mold and deckle.

The mold is a frame which has a mesh stretched tight across it. The deckle is an unmeshed frame of the same size which traps the pulp on the mold. These can be bought in craft shops or you can make a set from timber and nylon mesh. You will also need a basin large enough for maneuvering the mold and deckle. Basic instructions for making paper are given on the next page.

Once you have mastered the process, there are plenty of ways to experiment. Color can be added to the pulp in the form of tinted paper scraps or dyes. Petals and small leaves can be thrown in to create interesting textures. In Project 24, onion skins are processed and combined with the pulp to add both color and texture to cards.

Papermaking is fun and easy, and a piece of handmade paper is an excellent backdrop for pressed flowers or for more solid natural objects arranged as samplers.

Handmade paper made from white waste paper with (from left to right) onion skins; yellow envelopes and small leaves; food coloring and petals.

You can use the leaves and stems of long-fibered plants such as celery as a pulp base. Cut the material into 1 " pieces and boil it for two hours. Rinse well then blend as for paper. Tougher plants may need to be boiled with soda ash or caustic soda. Small amounts of plant matter such as onion skins can be boiled, blended, and added for extra interest.

To recycle waste paper, tear it into small scraps and soak in water overnight. Place a handful of scraps in a blender and fill it two-thirds with water. Blend for ten to fifteen seconds. Half fill a basin with water and add six batches of pulp. Prepare a couching mound by placing a damp cloth on a folded towel.

Stir the mixture. Hold the mold mesh-side up with the deckle tightly on top. Dip the mold and deckle vertically into the basin, level them under the surface and lift them straight up to catch a layer of pulp in the mesh. While water drains through the mesh, agitate the mold and deckle gently from side to side to even out the pulp.

Remove the deckle and tip the mold so that the paper lies on the couching mound. Roll away the mold, ensuring that no pulp sticks to it. Cover the sheet with a damp cloth and repeat the process. Press the layers of paper and cloth between weighted boards overnight. Hang each cloth-and-sheet to dry. When dry, peel paper off the cloth.

Leaves

Although flowers are usually considered the star attraction, nature rarely misses an opportunity to show off, and the variety of forms and colors found in leaves is a great demonstration of this. Many change further with the seasons, making fall almost as colorful as spring.

Evergreens were once thought to have magical properties because they retain their leaves throughout the winter months. Long before the popularity of the Christmas tree spread from Germany, branches of mistletoe were hung indoors for good fortune during the Yuletide in the depths of winter.

Holly and other evergreens are still wonderful additions to a winter display, whether it is a welcome wreath on the door, a swag over the fireplace, or a simple ring of greenery around the candle at the dinner table.

Foliage can be preserved by soaking it in a glycerin solution. This often affects the color of the leaves, turning them a rich brown or olive, but it keeps them supple and they retain their natural sheen. Leaves treated in this way are ideal for use in pots of dried flowers, topiary designs, or other lasting arrangements.

Pressing is another effective way of preserving leaves as both the color and the form are retained. Pressed leaves can be displayed between glass in hanging decorations, or framed in the window of a three-panel greeting card (see page 157). Glue overlapping leaves onto plywood pieces and apply several coats of polyurethane varnish to create sturdy coasters or place mats.

Many leaves contain a skeleton of veins and a midrib which are revealed when the softer epidermis rots away. You might find leaves in this lacy condition in early winter, but you can also skeletonize fresh ones yourself by following the instructions on the next page. Spray some gold or silver afterward for an especially beautiful effect.

Leaves offer plenty of scope in paint crafts as they make ideal blocks for printing, stencils for spattering around, and even bases for crayon rubbings.

Arrange delicate pressed or skeletonized leaves between two sheets of thin glass and clip them together or bind the edges with copper foil.

▶ Glycerin can be used to preserve stems of foliage and individual leaves. Split or crush any woody stems. Mix a solution of one part glycerin and two parts very hot water. Stand stems upright in this for four weeks or until the leaf color changes. Steep individual leaves in the solution for a week, then rinse and dry them.

◀ Pressed leaves are paper thin but retain their color and shape well. Choose leaves that have recently fallen or are still on the tree. Place them in a single layer between pieces of blotting paper in a flower press (see page 11) or between sheets of newspaper under a stack of heavy books. Leave for at least three weeks.

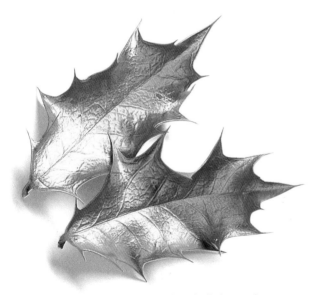

When holly leaves have dried out and lost their gloss, spray them with gold paint and they can be used as decorations indefinitely.

Leaf shadows
The natural skeletonizing process can be sped up. Mix 1 tbspn washing soda in 1 pint water. Simmer leaves in this solution for 30 minutes. Remove leaves with tongs and lay them on waste paper. Scrape the leaves with a knife. Mix 1 tbspn bleach with 1 pint water. Soak the leaves in this briefly and then rinse them well in water.

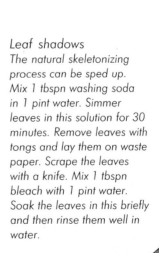

PROJECT 1

Pressed Leaf Box

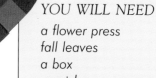

YOU WILL NEED
a flower press
fall leaves
a box
varnish
white glue
scissors
a glue gun
paper ribbon

The rich hues of fall leaves can be preserved by pressing and then enhanced with a coat of varnish. This is a stunning way to decorate an otherwise plain box.

1 ◄ Collect fall leaves which have not yet become brittle. Press them in a flower press or between the pages of a thick book for at least four weeks. Sort the pressed leaves by size and select the best ones.

2 ◄ Apply white glue to each leaf, spreading it evenly with your finger before fixing it in place. Glue a series of small leaves around the base of a round box. On the lid, glue a ring of overlapping leaves in contrasting colors. Make sure all parts of the leaves are glued down.

3 ► Spray the lid and the base of the box with several coats of gloss varnish, leaving it to dry between coats. Do this outdoors or in a well-ventilated room.

4 ► Cut a strip of paper ribbon and untwist it but do not flatten it fully. Roll it into a tight coil, glue the end and then fix this onto the lid with a hot glue gun. Glue another piece of untwisted ribbon around the edge of the lid.

PROJECT 2

Bay Leaf Balls

These decorations make great use of bay leaves, or any other sturdy leaf that dries well. You can use the leaves when they are fresh and flexible, or dry and dark.

YOU WILL NEED
bay leaves
a polystyrene ball
a marble
wire
wire cutters
gold paint
a knife
a glue gun

1 Make lots of small staples by bending the wire into a U-shape and then cutting it. Use a knife to gouge a hole in the polystyrene ball, large enough to accommodate the marble. The marble acts as a weight in the base of the ball.

2 Pick plenty of bay leaves in a variety of sizes and wipe them clean. Paint a handful of these gold. Apply gold paint to one side of the marble and to the top of the ball, opposite the hole.

3 Sort the leaves by size: small ones are needed for the top and base. Position a leaf so that the tip is at the top of the ball and fix it with a staple near its stem. Staple leaves around the ball. Dab glue onto the ball to secure the top of each leaf.

4 Work down and around the ball, stapling leaves and gluing the tips over earlier staples. Glue small leaves around the base and check that no areas of the polystyrene ball are visible.

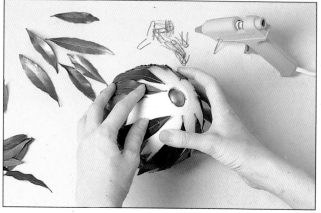

PROJECT 3

Ivy Cushion

This classical garland of ivy would also make an attractive tablecloth. Green is the natural choice, but you can select a different hue to match your furnishings.

YOU WILL NEED
linen or cotton
backing fabric
dressmaker's chalk
a plate or hoop
fabric paint
a brush
ivy leaves
decorative cord
cushion filling
sewing equipment

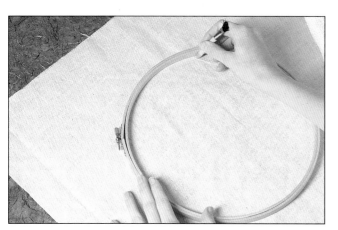

1 Cut two 12" squares of linen or cotton fabric. Lay a large plate or embroidery hoop on one piece of fabric and mark a faint circle in chalk. Select several ivy leaves of varying sizes and in good condition.

2 Brush fabric paint thinly on the face of a leaf and lay it face down on the fabric. Place scrap paper over the leaf, smooth it down with your fingers, then lift the leaf. Repeat this process, printing a series of leaves angled in and out of the circle.

3 Cut two 12" squares of backing fabric. Zigzag the edges of all four fabric squares to prevent fraying. Lay the printed square face down on the other linen square and sandwich these between two backing squares. Sew the four pieces together allowing a ½" seam and leaving a 4" opening.

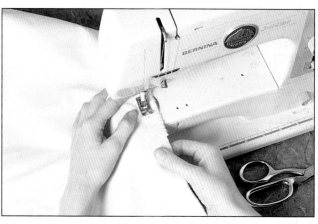

4 Trim the corners at an angle and turn the cushion right side out. Press it with a warm iron to cure the paint and remove any creases. Hand sew a decorative cord around the edges. Fill the cushion with plenty of stuffing and stitch the opening closed.

Nuts & Cones

The seeds and seedheads of trees take a multitude of forms and most of them can be used to decorate a house or to make ornaments. The textures and shapes of cones, pods and nuts provide an interesting contrast when added to a display of dried flowers. Pine cones strung with winter twigs make an eye-catching mobile. A stack of large cones looks attractive in the grate of an unused fireplace. A twig or willow basket filled with nuts makes a delightful centerpiece on a table.

Nuts and cones look delightful on wreaths and swags. They can be fixed in place with a glue gun; wiring each piece separately may be time consuming but gives greater control and creates a more durable result. Instructions are on the next page.

If you are lucky enough to have a plentiful supply of small cones, such as fir or larch, you can make a cone tree by wiring and attaching each cone around a dry foam base. A cone-shaped base, available from craft shops, gives you a tree in the traditional Christmas shape, or you could use a foam ball to create a tree akin to Project 27. Use cones which are quite dry or they will swell as the "leaves" open up; keep the finished project away from damp or the reverse will occur. Fill the gaps between the cones with moss.

Cones and nuts look stunning when sprayed with a light coat of silver, gold, or even white spray paint. Allow some of the natural color to show through the paint, creating a frosted effect. This is a particularly good way to give an old arrangement a second lease of life.

Small varnished acorns, hazelnuts, and nutmegs make interesting jewelry. Cap them with circles of leather threaded on thonging to retain a natural color scheme.

Cones and the hulls or shells of nuts were once a valuable source of natural dye. Walnut hulls produce a rich brown; pine cones offer up a reddish-yellow dye. Break up the cones or nuts into small pieces and boil them for several hours to release the color. There are plenty of delicious ways to use the contents of nutshells!

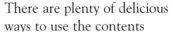

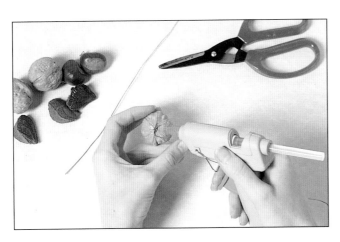

Bend the tip of a length of wire. Attach the bent end to a nut with a hot glue gun or fast-drying glue.

To wire a cone, bend a length of fine wire in half and loop it under the stiff "leaves" at the base of the cone. Twist the wire tightly to secure.

A touch of varnish and a binding of gold string can turn a large nut into a tree decoration.

Miniature pine cones and varnished hazelnuts nestle in oakmoss on this charming box lid.

PROJECT 4

Almond Delights

YOU WILL NEED
ground almonds
icing sugar
orange blossom water
halved walnuts
a mixing bowl
a teaspoon
wax paper

These simple sweets are a traditional Middle Eastern treat and will have special appeal for anyone who likes the taste of marzipan.

1 In a large bowl, mix 1 cup ground almonds and 1 cup sifted icing sugar. Add 3 or 4 tablespoons of orange blossom water (sometimes known as eau de fleur d'orange) or enough to make a stiff paste.

2 Knead the paste with clean hands until it is quite smooth. Leave it to rest for five minutes. Wash your hands and dry them thoroughly.

3 Sprinkle sifted icing sugar on a smooth surface. Take teaspoonfuls of paste and roll each one into a ball. Roll these in icing sugar and place them on a piece of wax paper.

4 Decorate the sweets by pressing a halved walnut into each ball. Leave them to dry out overnight. Store in a small box or tin, placing them in paper cases for an attractive presentation.

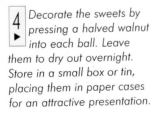

PROJECT 5

Nut Wreath

YOU WILL NEED
wreath base
unshelled nuts
leaves
glycerin
acrylic varnish
a brush
a glue gun
wire-edged ribbon
wire

A garland of nuts and preserved leaves is ideal for decorating the house throughout the winter, although it may not last the season if there is a nutcracker handy.

1 ▶ Apply a coat of gloss varnish to hazelnuts or chestnuts to bring out the colors. Make a solution of one part glycerin and two parts very hot water. Preserve ivy leaves by steeping them in this solution for a week. Alternatively, apply a coat of varnish to fresh leaves and allow them to dry out.

2 ▶ Apply hot glue to the back of the ivy leaves and glue them at intervals around a wreath base. If the base you are using is unattractive, cover it completely with leaves.

3 ▶ Work around the wreath, attaching nuts with dabs of hot glue. Position the large nuts first and use the smaller ones to fill any gaps. Make sure they are all securely fixed in place.

4 ◀ Tie a bow from a length of wired ribbon. Push a piece of wire through the center of the bow and bend it to form prongs. Attach this to the base of the wreath. Turn the wreath over and attach a loop of wire for hanging at the top.

PROJECT 6

Festive Branch

YOU WILL NEED
long twigs
moss
holly sprigs
small cones
gold spray paint
a glue gun
scissors
string
assorted ribbons

Here is an unusual idea for decorating a door at Yuletide. You can add anything you choose to it, but small cones sprayed with gold look especially festive.

1 Collect small pine or larch cones or buy them in bulk from craft suppliers. Apply a coating of gold spray paint and allow them to dry. If the cones are quite large and heavy, you may need to twist a wire around the base and attach them to the branch with this. Small cones can be attached with hot glue.

2 Gather thin branches or long twigs. If you cannot find any with moss or lichen already attached, twist clumps of dried moss around them. Bind the stems together tightly with string and cover the ends by gluing a clump of moss over them.

3 Cut a length of red ribbon and thread one end through the twigs below the binding. Knot the ends of the ribbon to form a loop and conceal the knot among the stems. Make a large bow from another piece of ribbon and glue it over the bound stems.

4 Use a hot glue gun to attach sprigs of holly leaves onto the twigs. We have glued tiny cones onto the holly. Attach the gold cones to the branch, as well as small bows made of red or tartan ribbon. Hang the finished arrangement by the ribbon loop.

Seeds & Spices

There is something about seeds that appeals to the child in us. It may be the bright colors, or perhaps curious shapes, or it may simply be the sheer quantity of them.

Such variety and bounty calls out to be put on display. Sampler boxes—the one below is a slide box—look wonderful with compartments of different seeds and spices. Jars can be filled with layers of grains and pulses, making an ideal decoration for kitchen shelves. Mosaics require more time and care but are enjoyable to craft.

Seeds are invaluable for making simple percussion instruments. Whether you fill a glass jar with rice or make elaborate papier-mâché maracas filled with pulses, the results will be entertaining.

Large seeds, such as those from pumpkins and sunflowers, can be drilled and threaded to make inexpensive jewelry. If the seeds are first dipped in gold paint, such pieces can look quite sophisticated.

Whatever spices lack in color, they make up for in scent. Place a few vanilla beans in a container with notepaper, seal it, and store it for a month before making a gift of the scented stationery.

Many spices also have intriguing shapes. A potpourri of star anise, coriander, cardamom, and juniper berries, with some small cones for bulk and a few drops of patchouli oil makes a wonderfully fragrant and attractive mix.

Cinnamon sticks are both fragrant and appealing to the eye. Tie small bundles of them with raffia, string, or a narrow ribbon and add them to wreaths, swags, or to the boughs of the Christmas tree.

Spices are, of course, valued highly for their flavor. Small bundles of muslin filled with a mix of cinnamon, nutmeg, and cloves, and tied tightly with cotton make a delicious drink when steeped in warmed wine.

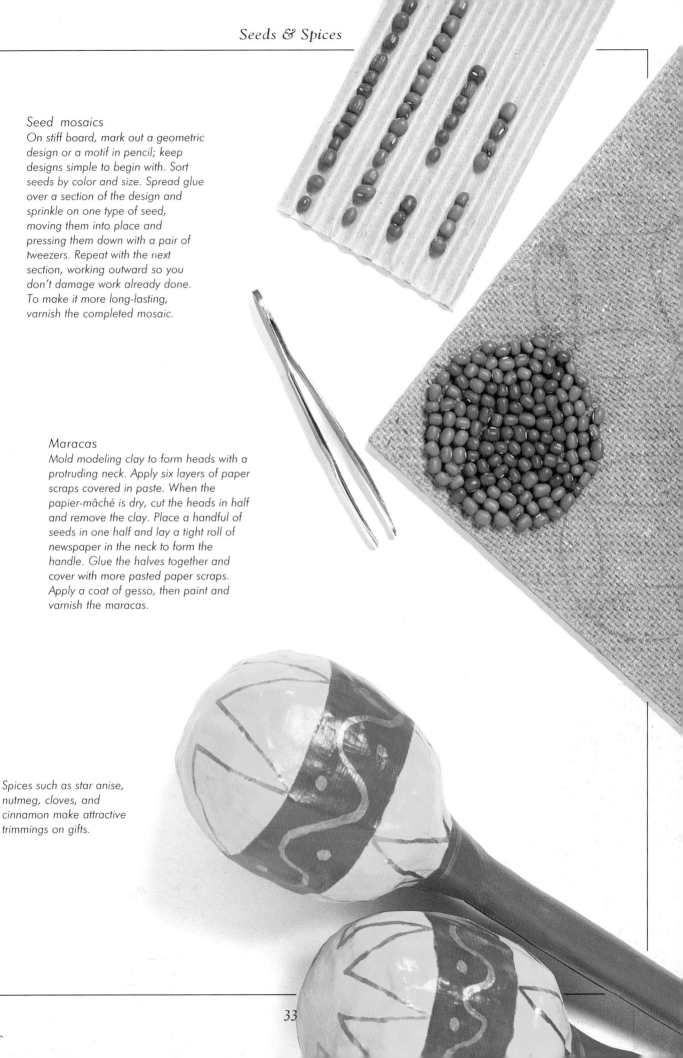

Seed mosaics

On stiff board, mark out a geometric design or a motif in pencil; keep designs simple to begin with. Sort seeds by color and size. Spread glue over a section of the design and sprinkle on one type of seed, moving them into place and pressing them down with a pair of tweezers. Repeat with the next section, working outward so you don't damage work already done. To make it more long-lasting, varnish the completed mosaic.

Maracas

Mold modeling clay to form heads with a protruding neck. Apply six layers of paper scraps covered in paste. When the papier-mâché is dry, cut the heads in half and remove the clay. Place a handful of seeds in one half and lay a tight roll of newspaper in the neck to form the handle. Glue the halves together and cover with more pasted paper scraps. Apply a coat of gesso, then paint and varnish the maracas.

Spices such as star anise, nutmeg, cloves, and cinnamon make attractive trimmings on gifts.

PROJECT 7

Tick-Tack-Toe

YOU WILL NEED
thick card
a ruler
a pencil
a knife & mat
brown paper
tape
glue
narrow ribbon
seed pods

In the game of tick-tack-toe, two players take turns to place their tokens on the board: three of a kind in a row wins. This charming version comes in its own gift box.

1 ▶ Cut an 8½ " square of thick card. Cut a 1½ " square from each corner to create flaps. Lightly score along the flaps with a knife. Fold up the sides and tape to form a box base. Repeat this with a slightly larger piece of card to form a lid which will fit over the base.

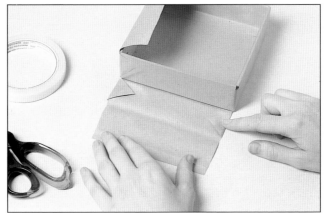

2 ◀ Cut a 12 " square of brown paper. Lay the box base in the center of the paper and cut darts in each corner of the paper. Cover the box base as shown, folding the darts around the corners of the box and gluing the flaps down. Repeat this for the box lid.

3 ◀ Cut a square of card which will fit into the box base and a larger square of brown paper. Cover the card with the brown paper, cutting darts at the corners and taping the edges down on the back. Cut four pieces of narrow ribbon and tape them on the back of the panel so they form a grid on the front.

4 ▶ Select suitable seed pods: you will need five each of two distinctive shapes. Pictured here are star anise and the spiky seed pods of liquidambars.

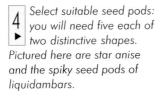

PROJECT 8

Beaded Cover

YOU WILL NEED
beans or seeds
netting or fabric
a drill
pliers
gold paint
a brush
scissors
a needle & thread
gold thread

Beaded jug covers were popular a generation or so ago, and they are still ideal for keeping the bees out of the lemonade on a warm summer's day.

1 ◄ Select 50 seeds of a reasonable size: we have used haricot beans. Drill a small hole in the top of each seed, keeping your fingers away from danger.

2 ◄ Divide the seeds into two piles; one pile will remain unpainted. Hold the seeds in place with a needle or long pin and apply a coat of gold paint. When the paint is dry, turn the seeds over and paint the other side.

3 ► Cut a circle of netting or open-weave fabric with a diameter of 8 " or whatever size suits the jug it will be used to cover. Moisten your fingers and roll the edge of the fabric slightly, stitching a narrow hem around the circle in a matching thread.

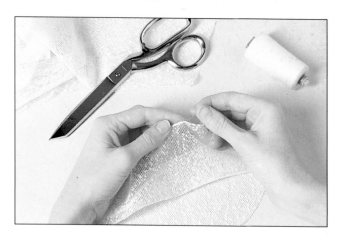

4 ► Secure a gold thread and sew several hemming stitches. Thread on a seed and sew another stitch, so that the seed hangs loosely. Sew three or four more stitches and attach another seed, alternating painted and plain seeds around the cover. Knot the thread and trim the end.

PROJECT 9

Chili Strand

With its bright reds and greens, this Mexican arrangement makes an unusual decoration during the Harvest Festival. The chilis will dry and remain colorful all year round.

YOU WILL NEED
wire
a head of garlic
chili peppers
strong scissors
a skewer
raffia

1 ◄ Cut a piece of fine wire 16 " long. If you have used wire from a reel, straighten it out. Bind one end of the wire tightly around the neck of a large head of garlic.

2 ► Use a skewer or large needle to pierce a hole through the stems of the chili peppers. String the peppers onto the wire, arranging them so they fan around the wire. Twist the top of the wire into a loop.

3 ► Make a thin 3-strand braid of raffia (see page 13). Bend it into a loop and bind the ends with wire. Connect this to the hanging loop of the strung peppers.

4 ► Make a generous raffia bow and tie it around the wire, concealing it from view. Hang the strand by the raffia loop.

Stones & Sand

Stones may seem, at first glance, to have limited uses in craft: their solidity and strength prevents them from being easily shaped. These properties can be turned to advantage: stones will bear any weather and so are ideal for outside projects. Their weight makes them excellent candidates for door-stops and paperweights, as in Project 10.

Pebbles smoothed by river or sea can be painted freehand or with stencils, or used as the base for fine decoupage, in which small images are cut from paper, pasted on and varnished over. Children enjoy painting animal features on stones with acrylic paints and creating their own "pet rocks."

Rough but interesting pebbles can be polished in a commercial tumbling device. Such stones can also be bought already polished

and then made into bracelets, pendants, cuff links, or simply displayed in a glass bowl filled with water, which brings out the colors of the stones. Some semi-precious stones are linked by tradition to months of the year (see the catalog on the next page) and a gift of the appropriate stone makes a thoughtful birth-day or birth present.

Small attractive stones can also be used as counters in board games (if they are easily differentiated) or as tokens in such counting games as mancala, widely played in Africa.

Sand offers quite a different set of proper-ties with which to work. In some parts of the world there are naturally occurring colored sands, but white sand can also be dyed to take on other hues. Tinted sand can be used to make decorative bottles or jars (see Project 11) or to create pictures; sand art is practiced in Tibet and among native peoples of North America. Sand can also be used as a mold fo casting or candlemaking.

Sand patterns
Make a miniature sand-pit for contemplative doodling. The rake is made from matchsticks glued to pieces of dowel.

BIRTHSTONES

Various semi-precious stones and personal qualities are associated with the months or phases of the moon.

January
garnet
constancy

February
amethyst
sincerity

March
bloodstone
courage

April
crystal
purity

May
chrysoprase
grace

June
moonstone
confidence

July
carnelian
wisdom

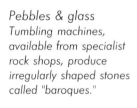
August
peridot
happiness

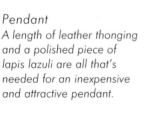
September
lapis lazuli
awareness

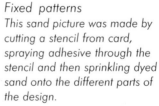
October
tourmaline
strength

November
topaz
fidelity

December
turquoise
prosperity

Pendant
A length of leather thonging and a polished piece of lapis lazuli are all that's needed for an inexpensive and attractive pendant.

Fixed patterns
This sand picture was made by cutting a stencil from card, spraying adhesive through the stencil and then sprinkling dyed sand onto the different parts of the design.

Pebbles & glass
Tumbling machines, available from specialist rock shops, produce irregularly shaped stones called "baroques."

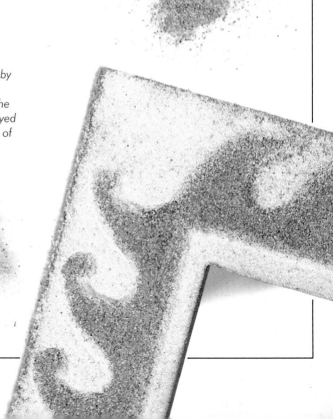

PROJECT 10

Paperweights

YOU WILL NEED
large pebbles
silver paint
black paint
brushes
a toothbrush
plain paper
a knife & mat

*River-smoothed pebbles make attractive paperweights,
especially when decorated with a monogram. Present one
to a friend with a set of sparkling stationery.*

1 ▶ Choose large, smooth stones which are stable and which have a flat surface. Paint each stone with several coats of acrylic paint, either in black or silver, and allow the paint to dry.

2 ▶ Dip the bristles of an old toothbrush in thinned paint and draw your thumb over the bristles to spatter fine specks of paint. Test this on scrap paper first: if the paint is too thick, the specks will be large. Spatter black paint on the silver stones and silver paint on the black.

3 ▶ Use a fine brush to paint one or more initials in the same color as the spatters. For a gloss finish, apply a coat of acrylic varnish when the paint has dried.

4 ▶ To make matching stationery, cut small sheets of plain white paper and spatter the edges with black and then silver paint. Do the same on the flaps of plain envelopes.

PROJECT 11

Sand Jars

Use natural pigments such as tea or coffee to dye sand and then create useful and attractive containers, showing off your work to good effect.

YOU WILL NEED
white sand
natural pigments
a sieve
a jar
a straight glass
newspaper
paraffin wax
kitchen equipment

1 Sieve white or pale sand to remove any debris. Divide the sand into several bowls. To each bowl, add a diluted pigment (such as filtered or instant coffee, tea, ground charcoal, or paprika). Spread the contents of each bowl on a separate newspaper to dry.

2 Choose a straight-sided glass which is narrower and shorter than your jar. Spoon white sand into the jar and sit the glass inside it so that the two rims are at the same level. Center the glass so that the gap between it and the jar is even all around.

3 Roll a square of paper into a cone shape, with a small opening at the point and secure it with tape. Trickle a layer of sand into the gap between the jar and the glass, using the paper funnel to control the flow and create a wavy pattern. Funnel the next layer in a different color and so on to create layers.

4 Melt a small amount of paraffin wax in a double boiler. Remove it from the heat and carefully pour it into the gap between the jar and the glass. If it overflows, wait until the wax has set and remove excess with a knife.

PROJECT 12

Birthstone Bracelet

YOU WILL NEED

tumbled stones
eyepins or thin wire
round-nosed pliers
wire cutters
jump rings
a clasp

A string of birthstones will become a treasured belong-ing later in a baby's life and so makes a wonderful christening or birth present.

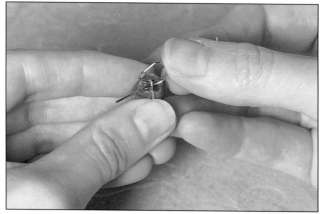

1 Select stones that are rounded rather than flat; see page 41 for a list of birthstones. Take an eyepin (or make a loop in one end of a piece of wire) and wrap it around a stone. Thread the end through the eye loop and bend the wire at a right angle: this is the top.

2 At the bottom of the stone, thread the end under the wire band and twist it to form a small loop, drawing the end once again under the band of wire.

3 Back at the top, draw the end through the eye loop and twist it back to form a second loop. Make sure the stone is now caged securely by the wire. Repeat this process until you have caged enough stones to form a small bracelet.

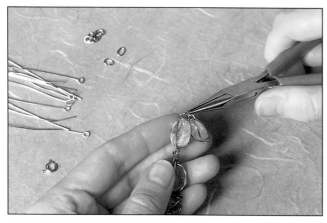

4 Open a jump ring (a ring of wire) sideways and thread on the top loop of one stone and the bottom loop of the other, then close the ring again. Link all the stones together in this way. Make sure that all jump rings have been pinched closed.

Suggestion: Eyepins and jump rings can be found at bead shops. Alternatively, they can be made by cutting and shaping fine, strong wire. Extra stones can be added as the child's wrist grows.

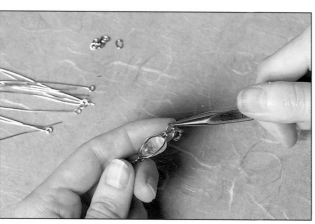

5 Secure a clasp to the first and last stones in the bracelet. We have used a bolt ring, but snap or screw fasteners are also suitable.

Eggs & Feathers

Eggs are a universal symbol of rebirth: both their contents and their shape suggest the cyclical nature of life. The decoration of eggs at springtime is a world-wide folk craft, and a far more enjoyable pastime than the giving of manufactured chocolate eggs.

Before you choose your method of decoration, you'll need to decide whether the eggs are to be eaten later, in which case you must use non-toxic dyes or paints, or whether you will boil the egg or blow out the contents. For an indefinite lifespan, eggs must be boiled slowly for half an hour. Instructions for blowing eggs are on the next page. To make blown eggs less fragile, block the base hole and carefully fill them with plaster of Paris or some other substance which will set.

Once prepared, eggs can be dyed, painted, marbled in a bath of oil paints floating on water, covered with pressed flowers, dyed and then engraved, treated to the techniques of batik, or decorated in a variety of other ways. To hang a blown egg, thread a ribbon through the holes and tie a knot at the base. Eggs can be hung singly or in a mobile.

The delicate forms of feathers have an intense appeal to the human eye, and feathers have been used in decoration in many cultures. In countries as diverse as Britain and China, small feathers were trimmed and arranged to create detailed pictures of birds and butterflies. American Indians use feathers in abstract arrangements which signify certain characteristics and have specific spiritual powers.

Feathers can be used in craft either as a tool for writing, painting, or printing, or as a basic material for adorning clothing and making jewelry and ornaments. Large feathers are often found when beachcombing or trekking. Quantities of feathers can sometimes be acquired from farms, poultry shops, mailorder businesses, or even from old feather dusters!

Make a small hole in the top and base of an egg with a pin and enlarge the holes with a skewer. Poke the skewer well into the egg so that the yolk breaks. Blow into the top hole and collect the contents in a bowl. Rinse the egg well by submerging it in water and leave it to drain on a paper towel.

Color eggs by submerging them in a dye bath (see page 12) until they are the desired hue. Blown eggs will need to be weighted down: a glass fitted in a jar will hold the eggs under the surface of the dye.

Onion eggs
Lay brown onion skins on a square of cloth and sprinkle with uncooked rice. Place a fresh egg on top, wrap the cloth around it and bind this with rubber bands. Boil for thirty minutes and allow to cool before removing the wrapping and rubbing the egg with cooking oil.

Earrings
Feathers and semi-precious stones such as turquoise make a stunning combination. These earrings are based on ornaments crafted by North American Indians.

Pysanki
These blown eggs have been decorated by Czech artists. Colored wax has been painted onto the dyed or uncolored eggs with a drawing tool called a "stuzka."

PROJECT 13

Quill Pens

YOU WILL NEED
feathers
a knife or scalpel
an emery board
a cutting mat

Quill pens were the main instrument for writing for some twelve centuries. They may have been superseded for every-day use but they are still a pleasure to use for calligraphy.

1 ▶ *Select a large wing feather with a hollow shaft that tapers to an almost closed tip. Cut off the very tip. Scrape the transparent cuticle from the shaft with your nail. Clean out the pith from the dent in the back of the shaft.*

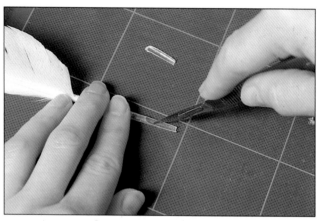

2 ▲ *Hold the feather in your hand to find the angle at which the pen should be shaped. Rotate the feather so that the underside is on top. Make a long cut which starts vertically and then slopes down to the tip, creating a scooped out section in the shaft.*

3 ▲ *Remove any pith from inside the shaft. Cut a full-length slit down the center of the nib: this creates a reservoir for holding ink.*

4 ◀ *Slope the shoulders of the scooped section so that the sides taper to meet at the center slit.*

5 ◀ *Cut straight across the point to create a nib of a suitable width: for broad pen strokes, cut a stubby nib; for general writing, cut a narrower nib. Sand the shoulders of the pen gently with a very fine emery board. You can re-nib the pen after it is worn from use.*

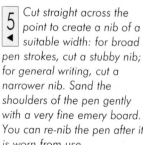

PROJECT 14

Easter Eggs

There are many ways to decorate eggs for Easter; here is one with a natural touch. For edible creations, you can dye the eggs with a vegetable dye and then hardboil them.

1 ▶ *Make a small hole in the top and base of an egg with a pin and enlarge the holes with a skewer. Poke the skewer well into the egg so that the yolk breaks. Blow into the top hole and collect the contents in a bowl. Rinse the egg well by submerging it in water and leave it to drain on a paper towel.*

2 ▶ *Gather a selection of small leaves or sprays of leaves. Dab vegetable oil onto the egg to hold the leaves in position. Smooth the leaves down so they lie flat against the egg.*

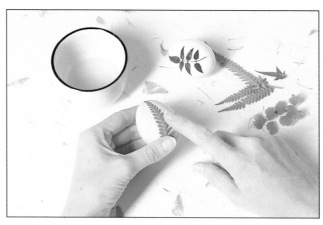

3 ▶ *Cut the legs off a pair of old stockings and tie a knot in one end. Carefully place the egg in the stocking tube and secure it with another knot. In a bowl or jar, add hot water to a dye. Fabric dyes produce a strong color; alternatively see page 12 for ideas on natural dyes.*

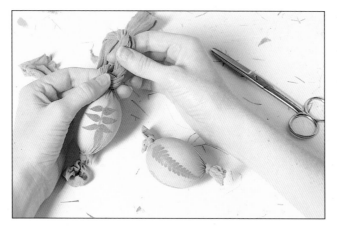

4 ▶ *Submerge the egg in the dye bath for 30 minutes. A glass which fits inside the neck of a jar will push the eggs below the liquid level. Remove the egg from the dye bath, cut the stocking away and lift off the plant material. Leave the eggs to dry on a paper towel.*

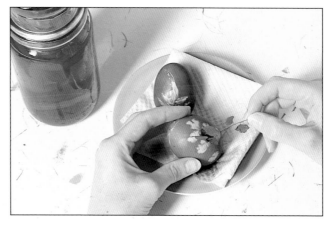

PROJECT 15

Lampshade

The delicate form of feathers is shown off beautifully in this project. These ones have been pulled from an old feather duster and given new life on an inexpensive lamp.

YOU WILL NEED
thick paper
thin paper
a lampshade frame
a knife & mat
a pencil
glue
a toothpick
spray adhesive
raffia or ribbon

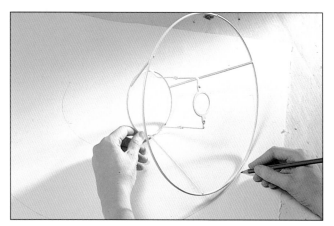

1 Lay the lampshade frame on a sheet of thick paper. Slowly roll the frame and mark the lines of both edges to map out the lampshade shape. Allow a 1" overlap at one end. Cut out this shape. Cut tissue paper or thin handmade paper to the same shape, but 1" larger all around.

2 Wrap the thick paper shape around the frame and glue the overlapping ends to form a shade. Apply a small amount of glue to the spine of a feather and glue it onto the shade. Glue feathers randomly around the shade.

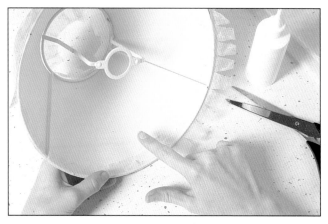

3 Spray some adhesive onto the tissue section and roll it onto the shade, making sure it lies smoothly. Cut darts in the tissue paper at the top and bottom of the shade. Place the shade on the frame, fold the darts over the wire and glue them on the inside of the shade.

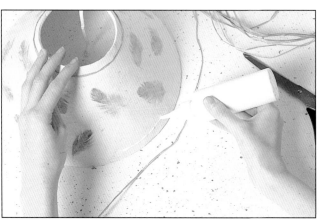

4 Measure and cut pieces of raffia or narrow ribbon to trim the top and bottom of the shade. Apply a line of glue and hold the trim in place until the glue has set. We have used raffia dyed with coffee (see page 89).

Shells

A stroll along the beach collecting empty shells is a relaxing pastime and one which never fails to amaze. The best time for such an exercise is at low tide, especially after a storm. Take care, however, that you are not breaking local restrictions: some countries prohibit the removal of natural items from the shoreline. You can also buy some discarded shells, including scallops and mussels, from fishmongers. Shell shops and mail order businesses are another source, but try to avoid purchasing shells which have been harvested live. Shells in imperfect condition are less likely to have been collected live, and the flaws don't diminish their beauty.

Clean shells by soaking them in water with just a dash of household bleach added. Thin shells should be soaked in this solution for only a few minutes, while large ones can be left for up to an hour. Rinse out the shells thoroughly in water.

Many shells can be drilled with a fine drill bit or by twisting the tip of a sharp blade to create a hole. Don't make your holes too close to the edges or the shell may break. Shells can be varnished to bring out the natural hues or painted with watercolors and varnished for an interesting effect. A hot glue gun is an efficient way to fix shells onto another surface or to glue shells together.

Most of the shells you find on the beach will be small in size. Bowls of such shells or simple framed arrangements both make attractive displays. They can also be drilled and used in jewelry, as buttons or simply as ornaments stitched onto clothing, accessories or furnishings. Medium size shells make delightful windchimes when drilled and strung in several chains. Large abalones make ideal soap dishes: they even have small holes which allow the water to drain out. Bivalve shells such as scallops and cockles were often hinged and used as needle cases or miniature jewelry boxes during the nineteenth century. Shells of all sizes can be embedded in acrylic resin as paperweights or combined in collages around a mirror, on a terracotta planter, or anywhere you choose.

For a fragrant display, wipe essential oil onto a piece of cuttlefish and arrange it with shells in a bowl.

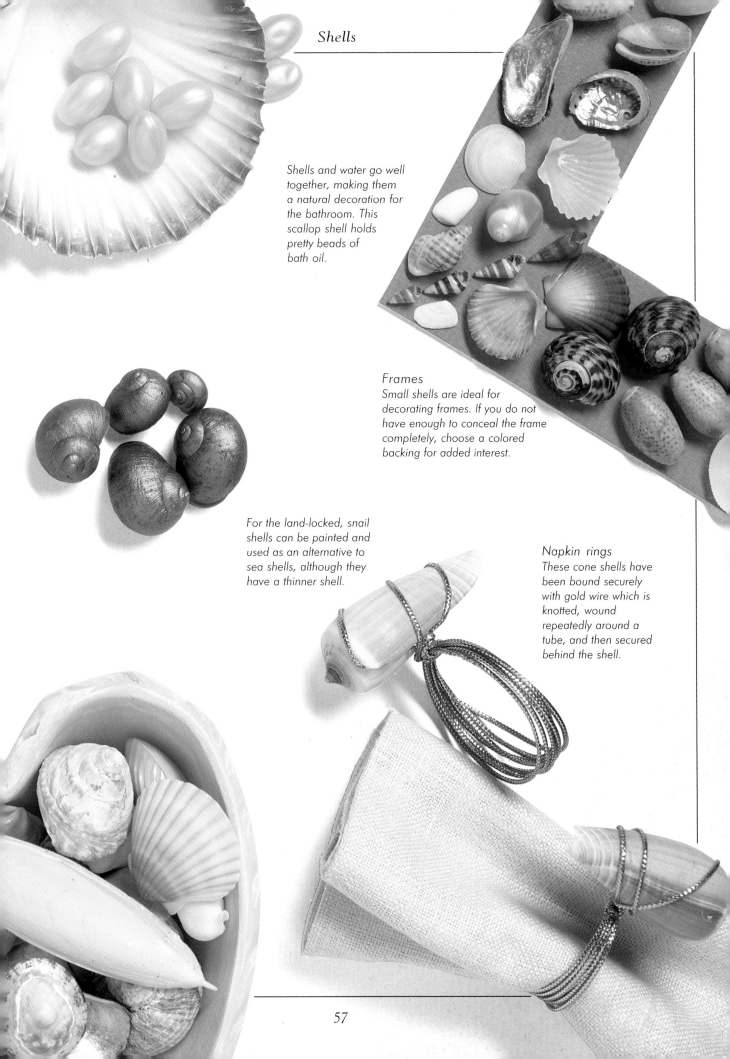

Shells and water go well together, making them a natural decoration for the bathroom. This scallop shell holds pretty beads of bath oil.

Frames
Small shells are ideal for decorating frames. If you do not have enough to conceal the frame completely, choose a colored backing for added interest.

For the land-locked, snail shells can be painted and used as an alternative to sea shells, although they have a thinner shell.

Napkin rings
These cone shells have been bound securely with gold wire which is knotted, wound repeatedly around a tube, and then secured behind the shell.

PROJECT 16

Shell Sampler

YOU WILL NEED
a picture frame
colored board
corrugated board
a knife & mat
a right-angle triangle
a glue gun

Display your collection of small shells in an attractive sampler. You could add a large shell in the center of the arrangement as a focal point.

1 ▶ Remove the glass from an old picture frame. Cut a piece of colored board to fit the frame. Cut four strips of corrugated board: two to match the width of the frame and two to match the height.

2 ◀ Use a right-angle triangle and sharp knife to miter the ends of the strips of corrugated board so that they fit neatly when arranged to form a frame. Fit the backing board and side strips in the recess of the frame and test for fit.

3 ◀ If the pieces are loose in the recess of the frame, cut four strips of card narrower and shorter than the mitered strips. Glue these around the edges and then glue the mitered strips on top. Refit the backing piece in the recess of the frame.

4 ▶ Arrange the shells in rows on the backing board before gluing them in place with a glue gun. To attach scallop shells, glue offcuts of corrugated board to the inside of each shell and glue these onto the backing.

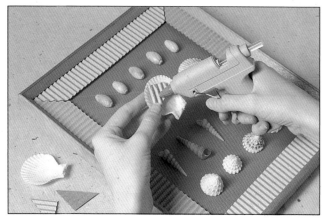

PROJECT 17

Scallop Necklace

YOU WILL NEED
a scallop shell
imitation pearl beads
a clasp
raffia
a drill
scissors

Seashells make beautiful adornments and there are shapes to suit every form of jewelry. Here is an idea for a necklace, complete with imitation pearls.

1 ▶ Select a large scallop shell which has both its shoulders intact. Drill three small holes along the edge of the fan and one in each of the shoulders.

2 ◀ Thread a thin piece of raffia through one of the three holes and tie a knot which secures it half way. Thread pearl beads onto the doubled raffia and knot the ends. Attach three beads from the center and two from each of the outside holes.

3 ▶ Thread a long piece of raffia in one shoulder hole and out the other and pull it so it is half way. Tie a knot at either side and then another a short distance from that. Thread three pearl beads on either side and tie a knot above them, then repeat this further up the raffia.

4 ▶ Check the required length by holding the necklace up to your neck. Thread the sections of a clasp on either end of the raffia and knot them securely. Trim excess raffia from the clasp knots and from the three strings of pearl beads.

PROJECT 18

Party Mask

Many shells have a beautiful luster on the inside but are otherwise quite unattractive. Here is one way to set off that sparkle to great advantage.

YOU WILL NEED
mussel shells
thick card
dowel
black paint
acrylic varnish
a brush
white glue
a knife
tweezers
spray adhesive

1 ◄ Rough out a mask shape on scrap paper and test it against your face for size. Copy it onto thick card and cut out the shape with a knife. Paint the mask black and then apply a coat of acrylic varnish. Paint a length of dowel in the same way.

2 ► Wash and dry mussel shells. Break them with your hands, or with a hammer if necessary. Break off small chips with tweezers, shaping them into rough squares by grinding material off the edges. Reserve the glitter that is created during this process.

3 ► Glue a series of chips around the edge of your mask, using the tweezers to position them neatly. Leave a narrow gap between each chip of shell.

4 ► Cut two holes in a piece of scrap paper so that part of the mask is visible beneath the paper. Spray a light coat of adhesive around the eye holes and then sprinkle the glitter onto the adhesive. When the front of the mask is dry, glue the dowel onto the back at one side as a handle.

Flowers

Flowers, whether from the garden or the markets, offer the craftsperson endless opportunities for producing beautiful and unusual projects. From simple fresh arrangements in a vase or more elaborate garlands and swags of dried flowers, to the subtle use of flowers in scented projects and cosmetics, there are any number of ways in which flowers can brighten our lives.

Fresh flowers should be picked before the heat of the day and the stems recut at a sharp angle then quickly placed in water and allowed a long drink before they are arranged.

To preserve their beauty, flowers can be dried in a variety of ways. They can be left to dry out naturally, either by standing them in a shallow amount of water, hanging them upside down or by laying flower heads on a wire rack. The drying process can be sped up by burying flower heads in a desiccant such as silica gel crystals, alum, or fine sand.

As they have a long lifespan, it is worthwhile arranging dried flowers in more complex projects. Delicate flowers may need to be wired before they are added to such displays, as will clusters of flowers with small heads. Wired flowers can be inserted into a foam base, while a glue gun or binding wire can be used to secure flowers to less solid bases made of twig, vine, or raffia.

In the art of potpourri (which incidentally means "rotten pot"), dried petals are blended with spices and fixatives, plus a few drops of essential oil, to make a fragrant and attractive mixture. Project 19 gives you an introduction to this traditional craft.

One of the most pleasing ways of treating flowers is to press them. Not only the petals but the leaves, buds, and roots can be preserved by thinning them with a sharp knife where necessary and then placing the sections between the pages of a thick book or between pieces of blotting paper in a press. Page 11 shows how to make a simple flower press; it is a valuable piece of equipment if your garden is well-stocked with flowers.

Many flowers are edible and were once considered delicacies. Rose petals, lavender, violets, and many other blossoms can be sprinkled over dishes or added to sandwiches. They can also be preserved with a coat of egg white and sugar and then used to decorate cakes and other sweet treats.

These dried rosebuds have been neatly halved so they sit flat on the card frame.

Crystallized violets have a long life and make a sweet addition to a dessert.

For hang drying, strip off
▲ unwanted leaves and
☐ bunch stems loosely,
staggering the flower heads.
Secure the bunch with an
elastic band. Bend the two
ends of a wire. Hook one
under the band and use the
other to hang the bunch.

☐ Spread some finely
▲ crushed desiccant in a
☐ box, rest the flower in it
and gently sprinkle more
desiccant into the flower head
and between petals. Seal the
box. Check regularly and
remove flowers when dry. Dry
the desiccant for re-use in a
low oven.

☐ Wire flowers for extra
► control and strength
☐ before adding them to
wreaths or swags. For hollow
stems, simply insert a wire.
For thin stems and sprays of
fine foliage, twist a wire
around the stalk. For larger
flowers, pierce the flower
head or calyx with a wire and
twist the wire around the
stem. If necessary, cover with
stem tape to conceal the wire.

Floral pomanders
Apply white glue to a
small foam ball and
roll it in dried lavender.
Glue pretty pressed
flowers on one at a
time. Arrange several
pomanders in a dish to
scent a room.

Pressed bouquet
Once pressed, flowers
can be reassembled and
arranged. This tiny posy
includes sea lavender,
larkspur, violets,
fuchsia, and yarrow.

PROJECT 19

Potpourri

A bowl of fragrant potpourri can add a decorative touch to a room while releasing a delicate floral scent. This recipe is based on that most popular of flowers, the rose.

YOU WILL NEED
fragrant roses
lavender
lemon verbena
orris root powder
cinnamon
cloves
essential oils
an airtight container
a display bowl

1 ▶ *Remove enough fresh rose petals to fill a large bowl and spread them on newspaper. Dry several whole roses and a bunch of lavender by tying the stems and hanging them upside down. Store these in a warm place for several days until they are dry. Remove the lavender florets and cut the heads from the whole roses.*

2 ▶ *In a bowl, combine 1oz orris root powder with ½ teaspoon cloves and 2 teaspoons ground cinnamon. Add four drops each of lavender and rose oil plus two drops of patchouli oil and mix the ingredients with your fingers.*

3 ▶ *In a large bowl, combine the dried rose petals and lavender with a handful of lemon verbena. Add the spice mixture and combine thoroughly. Put this mixture in an airtight container and lay the whole roses on top. Store this in a dark place for several weeks so that the scents develop fully.*

4 ◀ *Put the cured potpourri into a decorative bowl and arrange the whole roses attractively on top. When the scent fades, refresh it with a few extra drops of rose oil.*

PROJECT 20

Flower Pots

YOU WILL NEED
terracotta pots
lime wash
a brush
dry foam
a knife
dried flowers
dried moss
raffia

A colorful pot of dried flowers makes a thoughtful gift on Mother's or Father's day. A coat of lime wash gives a lovely chalky appearance to inexpensive terracotta pots.

1 Lime wash is a paint-like coating based on lime and is available commercially. Dampen the terracotta pot with water and apply a coat of lime wash with a wide brush. Allow to dry.

2 Cut and shape a piece of dry foam to fit your flower pot. If you cut too much off, wedge offcuts down into the gaps so that it fits well, with no movement.

3 Select dried flowers with a long and reasonably strong stem. Strip any lower foliage and trim stems to suit the pot. Insert them into the center of the dried foam, placing the stems close together. We have used lavender in one pot and delphiniums in the other.

4 Use a handful of dry moss to conceal the foam block. Cut the stems of other flowers, such as dried roses, and push them through the moss and into the foam so that they form a ring around the central bunch. Decorate the pot with a length of raffia, tied in a bow.

PROJECT 21

Bookmark

Bookmarks make thoughtful gifts and one decorated with
pretty pressed flowers is sure to be treasured. Instructions
for making a flower press appear on page 11.

YOU WILL NEED
a flower press
flowers & leaves
card
a cutting mat & knife
a ruler
ribbon
scissors
glue
a toothpick & tweezers
spray varnish

1 ▶ *Place fresh flowers and leaves in a flower press or between the pages of a large book, and leave them for at least three weeks. We have chosen pink larkspur, which keeps its color well, Queen Anne's lace, and ivy. The other bookmark pictured is decorated with fuschias and small beech leaves.*

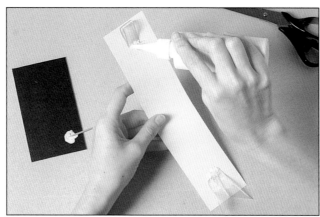

2 ◀ *Cut a strip of white or cream card, using a ruler and a sharp knife. Cut two pieces of ribbon with angled ends and glue them at the base so that they fan out. Cut another piece of ribbon, fold it in half and glue the ends onto the top section of the bookmark.*

3 ▶ *Plan the arrangement of the flowers before gluing them in place. Here, we have overlapped alternating larkspur and ivy, with florets of Queen Anne's lace adding interest. Use tweezers to handle delicate flowers and a toothpick to apply the glue.*

4 ▶ *Make sure all petals and edges are glued down. Give the bookmark a light coating of spray varnish. For extra protection, consider covering the bookmark with clear adhesive plastic.*

Herbs

Herbs are loosely classified as those plants which serve us, playing a role in medicinal or culinary endeavors or in other aspects of life. In some cultures, this description was, and is, extended to hundreds of plants. In many people's lives, it has dwindled to just a few common plants used to season food. This is a great pity, as an interest in herbs and their uses is a wonderful way of staying in touch with nature.

Herbs are generally easy to grow as they have not been hybridized as many flowers have. They can even be grown indoors or on windowsills, where they will provide a fragrant decoration. Evergreen herbs such as rosemary and bay can be grown in pots, clipped into topiary shapes, and decorated on festive occasions.

Many herbs dry well if they are tied in bundles and hung head down in a dark, dry place. Whether fresh or dried, they can be arranged in baskets, posies, garlands, or any display you choose.

Pressing herbs is another means of preserving them, and pressed herbs make beautiful decorations on cards, framed samplers, or sprinkled into the pulp when papermaking.

Some herbs yield up a dye when they are boiled: chamomile flowers produce a golden yellow while the sorrel root creates a soft pink. A mordant or fixative such as alum is usually needed to color materials permanently. Experimentation with herb dyes can yield wonderful results.

For those with culinary interests, herbs offer unlimited potential. A bottle of good quality oil or vinegar flavored with herbs makes a thoughtful gift. Soothing teas or tisanes can also be made from herbs, some of the most popular being chamomile, lemon verbena, and mint. For infusions with a stronger taste, a herb such as bergamot can be added to a China tea.

Herbs also have properties beneficial in cosmetics and can be used to make cleansing lotions, moisturizers, and hair treatments, all for a fraction of the usual cost.

Herbal oils
Basil, fennel, rosemary, tarragon, and marjoram are just some of the herbs that can be used to flavor cooking oils. Place fresh herbs and vegetable oil in a bottle and place it in a sunny spot for several weeks to steep.

Bouquet garni
These seasoning bundles can be made with fresh herbs or dried herbs which have been finely chopped. In a square of muslin, combine a bayleaf with sprigs of thyme, marjoram, basil, tarragon, and a little lemon rind. Tie the bundle tightly and leave one end of the string long enough to tie onto a saucepan handle.

Potted herbs
Miniature pots and half-pots are available from some craft shops. Fill them with fresh or dried herbs so you have a handy supply in the kitchen.

Lavender bags
Lavender, which is both colorful and fragrant, is also a moth-deterrent. Fill sachets with dried lavender to store among clothes and linen.

PROJECT 22

Bath Treats

Turn a bath into pure delight with a few natural ingredients. Fragrant bath salts, tap bundles, and soap sachets all combine to give skin a healthy treatment.

YOU WILL NEED
dried herbs
dried flowers
lavender oil
coarse oatmeal
coarse salt
plain soap
muslin
scissors
string
an airtight jar

1 ▶ *To make bath salts: measure 8 oz of coarse salt (also known as rock salt) and add 4 tablespoons of dried lavender and a few drops of lavender oil. Mix well and store in an airtight jar. Add 4 tablespoons of salts to hot running water for a soothing bath.*

2 ◀ *To make tap bundles: mix 2 parts dried rose petals, 2 parts dried lavender, 1 part dried thyme and 8 parts coarse oatmeal. Cut squares of muslin and place a large spoonful of the mixture in the center. Gather the corners and tie tightly with string. Tie a loop to hang the bundles under the hot tap of a bath.*

3 ◀ *To make soap bags: mix 1 part grated plain white soap, 2 parts dried herbs such as marjoram, thyme, or rosemary, and 2 parts coarse oatmeal. Stir the ingredients together.*

4 ▶ *Cut large squares of muslin and heap 4 tablespoons of the mixture in the center. Gather up the corners and tie the bundle very tightly with string. Rub the sachet over the body when bathing, avoiding areas of skin that are particularly delicate.*

PROJECT 23

Kitchen Wreath

YOU WILL NEED
fresh herbs
a hoop
thin wire
stem tape
strong scissors

This bright garland of green has a wonderful fragrance and can be ransacked during cooking, even once the herbs have dried.

1 Cover a number of wires with green stem tape: both of these items are available from suppliers of florists' materials. If stem tape is not readily available, you can use string or twine in place of wire to bind the herbs onto the hoop.

2 Find a wooden hoop or make a wire one by undoing and bending a coathanger. Bind on a piece of covered wire at two places to form a hanging loop.

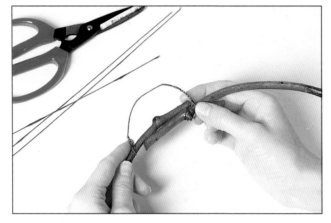

3 Collect a range of fresh herbs: those used here are red and green basil, rosemary, continental parsley, mint, and dill. Combine sprigs of different herbs in small bunches and bind the stems securely with fine wire.

4 Lay a bunch along the hoop and bind the stems on with taped wire or string. Lay another bunch over the stems and continue winding the wire around. Continue adding bunches, facing in the same direction, and binding them on, starting a new taped wire when necessary. Arrange the leaves for the best effect.

PROJECT 24

Herb Cards

The beauty of herbs is often overlooked, but when pressed and displayed on distinctive handmade paper they make eye-catching greeting cards.

YOU WILL NEED
fresh herbs
a flower press
white scrap paper
brown onion skins
a blender
a mold & deckle
a basin
kitchen equipment
a gold pen
glue

1 ▶ Collect sprigs of fresh herbs; those pictured are rosemary, marjoram, and sage. Lay the sprigs down and cut off any bulky leaves that prevent them lying flat. Place the sprigs and the separate leaves in a flower press or between the pages of a thick book and leave them for at least three weeks.

2 ▶ Tear white paper, such as old envelopes, into scraps and soak them in water overnight. Place a handful of scraps in a blender, fill it two-thirds with water and blend for ten seconds. Boil a handful of brown onion skins in water for an hour and then blend this mixture briefly. Half fill a basin with water, add six batches of pulp and the onion-water.

3 ▶ Follow the instructions on page 15 to form small sheets of paper. This involves dipping a mold and deckle into the pulp mixture, turning the sheets onto a bed of towels, pressing them, and hanging them to dry.

4 ▶ When the paper is quite dry, fold each sheet in two and run the back of your fingernail along the fold. Rule a border on the front of the cards with a gold pen. Glue a spray of pressed herbs on each card, adding extra leaves to recreate the original appearance.

Fruit

If you are lucky enough to have a fruit tree in your garden, you'll know the joy of having a glut of fruit at certain times of the year. Numerous kitchen crafts have developed, dedicated to preserving fruit for those times when the tree is bare and for creating variety in the ways they are presented.

Most of these crafts produce delicious edible fare and many of them make ideal gifts. Homemade preserves and jams are today such a rarity that they will be gratefully accepted. Fruit as diverse as figs, berries, peaches, and cumquats can be poached in a sugar syrup and then steeped in brandy, making a wonderful dessert base.

Some people can't go past a selection of crystallized fruit. Fruit is blanched in simmering water and then covered repeatedly, over a period of two weeks, with a heavy sugar syrup. When the pieces have soaked up enough sugar, pack them in a pretty box.

Toffee apples are much quicker to make and are an ideal treat for children at Halloween. Sugar, butter, water, and a dash of vinegar are mixed and heated to 290°F. Apples on sticks are dipped into this toffee and then into iced water to set.

There are also plenty of non-edible projects to make using preserved fruit. Pomanders, aromatic balls for scenting cupboards and drawers, can be fashioned from citrus fruit, as in Project 26. Citrus peel, dried in an oven on a low setting, is a wonderful ingredient in spicy potpourri mixes. Many fruits can be dried slowly in a low heat and eaten, or wired and used in decorations.

Many exotic fruits, such as star fruit, are especially decorative. Pomegranates, which grow in warm climates, preserve well and can look very festive. To dry them, cut a hole in the base and remove the seeds then fill the cavity with newspaper. Once they are dry, spray them lightly with gold paint, allowing the natural color to show through.

Fresh apples make a simple but delightful decoration when polished and tied with a piece of raffia. Whole apples can also be wired and added to large arrangements.

◀ Cut thin cross-section slices of oranges and apples. Add 1 teaspoon of salt to the juice of a lemon and soak the apple slices in this for a few minutes. Dry the slices with a paper towel. Place apple and orange slices in a single layer on trays and bake them on a low heat for several hours, turning them occasionally.

◀ To wire several slices of dried fruit, fan the pieces and push a wire through them all at the base, then twist the wire to secure. Single slices of orange look attractive when raffia is threaded through the center and knotted at the edge.

Fruit prints

Apples, citrus, star fruit, and many others can be used as printing blocks to make stunning and inexpensive giftwrap. Cross-section fruit neatly and mop up excess moisture with a paper towel. Place the cut face in the paint or ink and press it firmly onto clean paper. Re-coat the block before printing to ensure the image is the same each time.

Chocolate fruit

Dry segments of apple, mango, apricot, and other fruit in an oven on a low setting, or buy fruit that has been dried commercially. Dip the pieces in chocolate which has been melted in a double boiler to create delicious treats.

PROJECT 25

Apple Candles

Rosy red apples make delightful candle holders to sit on the table or float among leaves and petals: an ideal arrangement for a summer party held outdoors.

1 Polish the apples with a soft cloth and pull out the stalk. If you are using tea candles which come in metal cups, remove the cup and use the sharp edge to pierce a ring in the top of each apple. Otherwise, place the candle on top of the apple and use it as a template to cut a circle.

2 With a sharp knife, cut straight down into the apple. Make two cross cuts intersecting the circle and then cut out sections of apple.

3 Use a teaspoon to scoop out the flesh of the apple as necessary. Fit the candle in the depression so that the top lies flush with the top of the apple.

4 Place several apple candles in a glass bowl and slowly fill it with water. Scatter a few green leaves and bright petals on the water and place the bowl in position before lighting the candles.

NOTE: Do not leave any candles burning unattended.

PROJECT 26

Pomanders

Pomanders were carried centuries ago to ward off unpleasant odors and infection. Today, they fill a wardrobe or room with the tang of citrus and the rich aroma of cloves.

YOU WILL NEED

citrus fruit
cloves & spices
essential oil
a skewer
masking tape
scissors
a paper bag
ribbon
a glue gun
embroidery thread

1 ▶ Wipe a piece of citrus fruit with an essential oil. Cut strips of masking tape slightly wider than your ribbon. Tape around a piece of citrus fruit twice so that it is divided into quarters.

2 ▶ Pierce the skin of the fruit with a skewer or large needle and insert a series of cloves in the areas not covered by tape. Leave a gap between each clove, as the fruit will shrink as it dries. Gently remove the tape.

3 ◀ In a bowl, mix equal parts of orris powder (a fixative available from craft suppliers), ground cinnamon, and nutmeg. Roll the clove-studded fruit in the spices, making sure that it is coated evenly. Place in a paper bag and store this in a dark, dry, airy cupboard for five weeks.

4 ◀ To make a tassel, first lay a piece of embroidery thread along a strip of card then wind extra thread around the card. Remove the card, bind the neck of the tassel and then trim the ends. Decorate the cured pomander by gluing ribbon in the gaps and tying a loop at the top and a tassel at the base.

PROJECT 27

Fruit Tree

Dried fruit is the main ingredient in this stunning example of topiary, giving the arrangement a delightful scent and a slightly exotic appearance.

YOU WILL NEED
a foam ball & block
a branch or vine
a terracotta pot
a glue gun
a sharp knife
florist's wires
strong scissors
raffia
fruit & nuts
cones & wheat

1 Dry apples and orange slices (see page 81) and collect other suitable materials: we have used dried tomatoes, fresh chili peppers, garlic heads, wheat, cones, and sprigs of herbs. You will need a surprisingly large amount of material to cover the foam ball.

2 Wire bundles of wheat, chilis, and herbs by twisting a wire around the stems. Wire the fruit by piercing several slices with a wire and twisting it securely. Tie raffia bows and twist a wire around each bow.

3 Shape a dry foam block so it will fit the pot. Apply glue from a hot glue gun inside the pot and fix the foam in place. Cut a section of branch or strong vine to form the trunk. Cut a hole in the foam block and the foam ball and then assemble the tree structure.

4 Insert wired bunches of wheat heads into the foam ball, spacing them at even intervals. Next, insert the wired raffia bows, turning the pot as you work.

5 Add the other wired materials, leaving the sprigs of herbs until last and using them to fill any remaining gaps. Glue a layer of chestnuts or other nuts around the base of the trunk so that the foam block in the pot is concealed.

Raffia

Raffia is harvested from the leaves of a palm which grows in the forests of east Africa. It is the outer skin of young leaves, dried to make long supple strands which are straw-colored, lightweight, and surprisingly strong. Single strands are known as "blades." Raffia is usually sold in large bundles which each contain enough blades for several projects.

Like many other fibers, raffia can be crocheted, braided, and knotted. It can be stitched on open-weave canvas. It can also be used to bind or wrap other materials, as in Project 28. This is a simple example of coil work, where a core of string or cane is simultaneously wrapped and coiled into a shape, either flat or three-dimensional. By introducing dyed raffia and experimenting with other stitches, you can create complex geometric patterns.

Raffia is a lovely fiber to braid, either as a base for a swag of dried flowers or a string of chilis, or as the first step in making a stitched article. It has a waxy coating which conditions the hands, and working a long braid can be very relaxing. Instructions for different types of braids appear on page 13. If you find your finished braid is somewhat misshapen and lumpy, cover it with a damp cloth and press it with a hot iron.

A raffia braid is the basic material for many wonderful projects such as hats, baskets, bowls, and boxes. In this type of raffia work, a long braid is stitched into a spiral. To make this possible, it is best to start with a thin braid and add extra blades gradually to form a braid of the appropriate thickness. Instructions for this, and for stitching the spiral, appear on the next page.

To keep a spiral flat, for say the top of a hat or the base of a basket, the braid should be eased or gathered as you stitch; if you do not do this, the spiral will develop a gentle curve. If you pull the braid tightly as you stitch, it will cause the spiral to slope steeply. These shaping techniques are especially important when you are forming a hat with its different planes for crown and brim.

Projects 29 and 30 offer examples of a hat and a basket. Once you feel confident working with raffia, you can experiment with other hat styles or make baskets with flat bases and shaped sides. You'll find plenty of friends will place orders!

Wire bows of raffia and add them to arrangements of dried flowers and grasses. Raffia can also be wound around washers to make earrings and pendants.

To dye raffia, coil a bundle loosely and tie it at several places. Add hot water to a chemical or vegetable dye (see page 10). Submerge the raffia into the dye bath and soak it for ten minutes. Rinse it and allow it to dry thoroughly.

Right: raffia dyed with (from top to bottom) food coloring, coffee, undyed, turmeric.

For a braid which will be stitched into a spiral, start with only 10–15 blades. Bind the ends together and tie this to something fixed to give tension. Divide the blades into groups and follow one of the diagrams on page 13.

Add extra blades of raffia to replace old ones or to thicken the braid by laying the end along one strand of the braid and weaving another strand over it.

To finish the braid, thin it off by cutting out blades of raffia, or by not adding more, and continue until the braid is quite thin. Bind the ends and trim neatly.

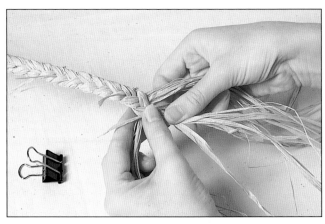

Thread a needle with a strong blade of raffia. Form a spiral by twisting the braid end sharply and winding the rest of the braid around in a tight coil. Make small overhand stitches to secure the spiral.

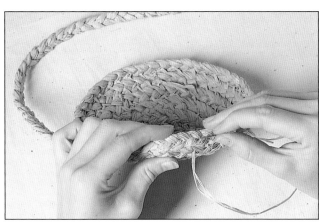

PROJECT 28

Coasters

YOU WILL NEED
sisal rope
raffia
scissors
a tapestry needle

These coasters are an example of coiled work, in which a core material is wrapped and stitched into a tight coil. Lazy Squaw stitch, used here, is the simplest one to learn.

1 ▶ Measure and cut 4 ' 3 " of ¼ " sisal rope. Cut one end at an angle. Place a piece of raffia along the end, bend it, and wrap it around the rope, securing the raffia end at the same time. Wrap 1 " and then stop.

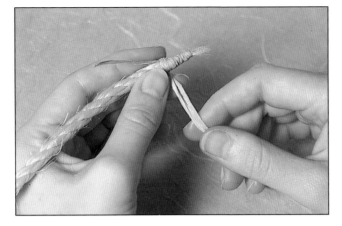

2 ▶ Thread a blunt needle, such as a tapestry needle, onto the end of the raffia. Twist the wrapped section of rope into a tight circle. Wrap the raffia several times so that the rope is secured in a ring.

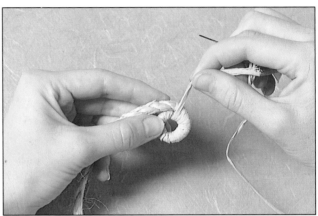

3 ◀ Wrap twice around the uncovered rope and then once around both it and the previous coil. Continue in this way, using the needle to pierce between coils when necessary and stitching in the gaps of the previous coil. Join in new raffia by laying a piece along the rope and wrapping around it for a few stitches before using it for wrapping.

4 ◀ As the coil gets bigger, add extra long stitches to make the coaster strong. To finish the coil, cut the end of the rope at an angle and bind it securely to the previous coil. Thread the end of the raffia back into the work and trim it.

PROJECT 29

Easter Hat

YOU WILL NEED
raffia
scissors
a tapestry needle
a tape measure

The Easter holiday is just the right amount of time to make this stunning raffia hat. The brim can be any style you choose and is shaped toward the completion of the project.

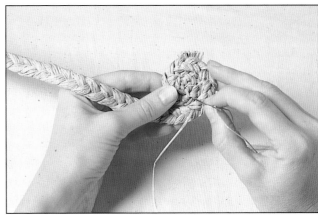

1 Start a 3-strand braid with five blades in each strand (see page 13). Add extra blades as you braid (see page 89) until it is ⁵/₈ " wide. Continue working the braid until it is at least 10 ' long. Braid the remainder later on as required.

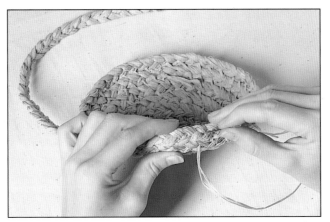

2 Trim the projecting ends from the braid. Thread a tapestry needle with a strong piece of raffia and stitch the braid into a coil as shown on page 89. Make sure the coil is stitched flat until it is 3 " in diameter or large enough for the top of your head.

3 When the coil is symmetrical, lean the braid over as you stitch so that it slopes gently. Test continually for fit as you stitch the sides. Continue stitching the crown until it reaches the tips of your ears.

4 When the crown is deep enough for your taste and appears symmetrical, lean the braid outward and stitch under the brim. Ease the braid as you stitch so that the coil is once again flat. Continue until the brim is the width you require.

5 Decide how you want to style the brim. For a rolled-up brim like the one pictured, stitch the last two rounds quite tightly and lean the braid upward. Thin down the braid when you near your completion point, and secure the end of the braid with extra stitches.

PROJECT 30

Flower Basket

YOU WILL NEED
raffia
dye
a bowl
scissors
a tapestry needle
a tape measure

This simple basket offers a wonderful companion for gathering flowers and herbs from the garden. The dyed raffia adds a touch of extra interest.

1 ▶ Coil a bundle of raffia loosely and tie it at several places. Add hot water to a chemical or vegetable dye such as food coloring, coffee, tea, or fabric dye. Submerge the raffia into the dye bath and soak it for 10 minutes. Rinse it and allow it to dry thoroughly.

2 ◀ Using undyed raffia, start a 5-strand braid with three blades in each strand (see page 13). Add extra blades as you braid (see page 89) until it is ¾ " wide. When the braid is 5 ' long, work in dyed raffia and continue for another 10 ', then braid with undyed raffia for another 10 '.

3 ◀ Trim any projecting ends from the braid. Stitch the braid into a flat coil (see page 89 for more detail). Thin down the braid by not adding new blades and finish it at a place where the coil will be symmetrical. Stitch the end of the braid onto the coil, securing the end with extra stitches and trimming it.

4 ▶ With undyed raffia, make a 3-strand braid approximately ¾ " wide. Work the braid until it is 5 ' long and then bind the end. Curve the coil and wind the braid around it twice so that it crosses in the front and meets again at the back. Pin it in place and stitch the handle onto the coil.

Straws

Straws refers to stems of grains such as oats, wheat, barley, and rye. The neutral colors of straws make them an ideal ingredient for arrangements of dried flowers, but there are other techniques for crafting with straws.

The braiding of straws into symbolic forms was practiced in ancient times wherever grain was harvested. These were thought to please the spirit that embodied the field, protect that spirit over the winter period, and to increase the fertility of the next year's crop. In the Middle East, ornate designs known as "Arabic cages" were woven. In Europe, small idols or "dollies" were crafted from the last sheaf to be harvested and set above the hearth until the next sowing, when it was carried back to the field and plowed back into the soil. As pagan influence weakened, this custom produced elaborate woven crosses, which were carried with ceremony to the church and displayed there.

Another traditional craft is split straw work, in which the ear of grain is removed, the straw split lengthwise, flattened, cut into shapes, and used for decoration. This technique was popular in Europe during the eighteenth century and is still a folk craft enjoyed in parts of the world today.

In Russia, boxes and platters are decorated with uncolored, geometric patterns. In China, amazingly fine pictures of birds and flowers are created with dyed and precisely cut straws. Split straw designs are especially eye-catching when worked on a black background, as in Project 33, when they look similar to marquetry. Simple split straw designs also look effective on eggs which have been dyed strong colors.

Bundles of straws, most commonly wheat, are available from many craft shops and from wholesalers who supply florists. Straws from the field should be picked two weeks before the harvest, otherwise grains will fall out while you are working with it. Pull off the long leaf and, before crafting them, soak the straws in water to soften the fibers. If you are storing straws for later use, keep them in a dry place as they will develop mold if damp.

From left: bearded wheat, oats, and quaking grass.

Garland of gold
Wreaths made of wheat are a
Christmas tradition in the
Slavic countries of eastern
Europe. This ring has been
formed by braiding the stems,
adding extra straws at regular
intervals, and then weaving
the ends in. Another method
is to cut the ears with a short
amount of stem, wire them in
bundles and insert these into
a circular foam base. Trim
with dried flowers if you want
a wreath with added color.

Mordiford dolly
There are hundreds of
traditional corn dolly shapes,
many of them named after the
region where they developed.
This one, from England, is
tied with a green ribbon
symbolizing new growth.

Napkin ring
A fine braid of straws can be
twisted into a rustic napkin
ring. See page 13 for basic
instructions on braiding.

PROJECT 31

Harvest Sheaf

YOU WILL NEED
a bundle of straws
wire or string
strong scissors
wire-edged ribbon

Celebrate the wealth of nature with a stunning sheaf of wheat
or other straws. This arrangement looks very attractive in an
unused fireplace or on a country dresser.

1 Strip off the loose leaves from the stalks and set aside a third of the straws. Bunch the remaining two-thirds so that the heads form a sphere. Bind the stalks with wire or string.

2 Holding the central bunch in one hand, add the extra straws at an angle as shown. Use wire or string to bind this outer layer so that it fans out neatly.

3 Make sure the heads are arranged to form a neat sphere. Trim the stalks to an even length so that the binding is roughly halfway down the stem. Test that the sheaf is stable when it stands and that it looks balanced: you may need to cut some or all of the stems shorter.

4 Tie a piece of wire-edged ribbon into a bow. Thread a wire through the middle and twist to secure. Poke the wire ends through the sheaf and secure at the back. Conceal the binding wire by wrapping a short section of ribbon around the stems and twist it to secure.

PROJECT 32

Straw Dollies

YOU WILL NEED

straws
cream thread
ribbon
scissors
a long container

You don't need to be a wheat farmer to have an excuse for making straw dollies. These delightful country tokens can be hung above a doorway for general good luck.

1 Select straws of wheat, oats, or rye which are at least 12 " from the base of the ear to the first leaf joint. Strip any leaves from the straws. Fill a long tray or tall jar with cold water. Soak the straws for an hour so they become flexible.

2 Gently wipe the straws with a cloth. With a piece of strong thread, tie three straws together just below the ears. Trim the ends of the thread close to the knot.

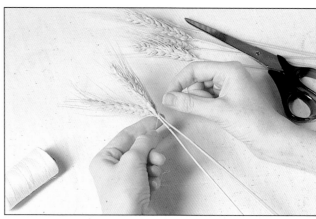

3 Braid the straws in a simple three-strand braid (see page 13). Secure the end of the braid with another knot of strong cream-colored thread.

4 Ease the braid into a lovers' knot as shown in the diagram. Tie the start and end of the braid together with a narrow ribbon.

Suggestion: The more complex dolly pictured is made by braiding three strands of three straws.

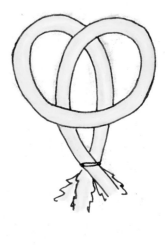

PROJECT 33

Mosaic Frame

This dramatic frame is decorated with split-straw work.
The result is well worth the effort required, but if time
is short, consider simplifying the design.

YOU WILL NEED
straws
black card
a ruler
a knife & mat
acrylic varnish
a brush
an iron
scissors
glue
a toothpick
tweezers

1 Measure the dimensions of your photograph. Cut a piece of black card with a window slightly smaller than the photograph and a border 2 " wide. Cut a back section the same size. Trace the pattern for the stand onto card, then cut along the solid lines and score lightly along the dotted lines.

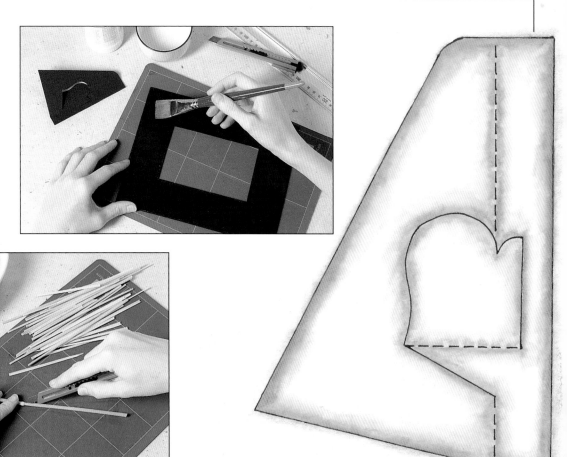

2 Soak a handful of straws (from wheat, barley, etc) in water for two hours. Remove any leaves. Split each straw lengthwise with a sharp knife. Place the split sections between two sheets of blank paper and iron flat.

3 Trim the flattened straws lengthwise so they are roughly the same width. Using scissors or a knife, cut the straws at an angle to form diamond shapes. If the straws are tending to crack lengthwise, cover the back with a strip of masking tape before cutting into diamonds.

4 Start at the middle of the frame and arrange the diamonds, making sure that the pattern will turn around the corners neatly. Apply glue to each diamond, position it with tweezers and press in place. Finish edges with narrow strips of straw. Apply a coat of varnish. Assemble the stand, backing, photo, and frame with glue.

Twine

In the days before the development of acrylics and other manufactured materials, rope and string were fashioned from natural plant fibers, or animal fibers such as wool. These items played an important part in daily life and in trade. For sailors, a well made and well secured rope could mean the difference between life and death so ropemaking, splicing, and knotwork were all serious crafts.

Today we have lost touch with the mythology of twine, but it does not take long to reacquaint yourself with the characteristics of these materials. Compare different types such as sisal, jute, coir, or cotton string: tease out fibers, try knotting and braiding it, or weaving it with other strands.

Macramé is the craft of knotting strands of yarn to create patterns. Most of the knots are extremely simple ones: the skill is in making sure that the patterns are balanced. The choice of yarn depends on the project. Fine string is suitable for jewelry or decoration on clothing. Medium yarns should be used for more practical items such as chair backs and seats, shopping bags and hanging baskets. Heavy cord is suitable for projects which must cope with wear: doormats, hammocks, rugs, and so on. Likewise, the love knot in Project 35 can be tied in different fibers for different effects: in a silken cord it makes a delicate adornment for a hairclip; tied in heavy sisal or seagrass, it makes a sturdy doormat.

String can also be crocheted and knitted. Feathers and beads can be added to crocheted chains of cotton string to create interesting jewelry. A mit or square knitted in fine sisal makes an excellent back washer: the coarse fibers remove rough skin and stimulate the circulation. Light-colored twines such as cotton and sisal take dyes well.

An even simpler way of working with twine is to wrap it around a solid object or coil it on a flat surface. Old tins, frames, and mats can all be rejuvenated with such a treatment. Items such as lampshades and booklets can be laced with a cord as a binding or simply for decoration.

*From left to right:
bleached cotton,
unbleached cotton,
sisal, jute.*

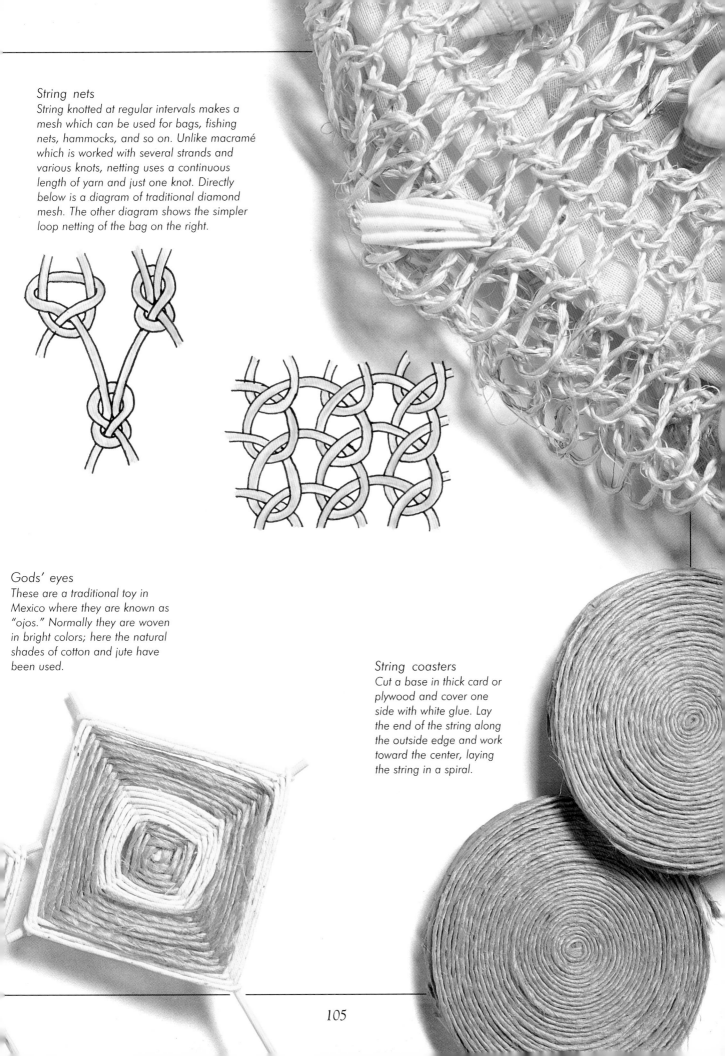

String nets

String knotted at regular intervals makes a mesh which can be used for bags, fishing nets, hammocks, and so on. Unlike macramé which is worked with several strands and various knots, netting uses a continuous length of yarn and just one knot. Directly below is a diagram of traditional diamond mesh. The other diagram shows the simpler loop netting of the bag on the right.

Gods' eyes

These are a traditional toy in Mexico where they are known as "ojos." Normally they are woven in bright colors; here the natural shades of cotton and jute have been used.

String coasters

Cut a base in thick card or plywood and cover one side with white glue. Lay the end of the string along the outside edge and work toward the center, laying the string in a spiral.

PROJECT 34

Classical Urn

YOU WILL NEED

a terracotta pot
white paint
a sponge
wet-&-dry paper
sisal rope
strong scissors
a glue gun
large clips
white glue

A few dabs of paint and a coil or two of rope are all that's needed to turn a plain terracotta pot into a container fit to grace any living room or courtyard.

1 Select a large terracotta pot with a plain shape. Moisten a sponge and dip it in white paint, such as gouache or acrylic. Dab any excess paint onto scrap paper and apply a light, uneven coat of paint onto the pot.

2 When the paint has dried, rub it lightly with a piece of wet-&-dry sand paper which has been soaked in water. This will give the pot a worn appearance.

3 Measure and cut a piece of sisal rope long enough to encircle the pot four or more times. Glue the rope onto the hip of the pot using a hot glue gun.

4 Cut pieces of sisal rope and coil one tightly with your fingers. Hold the coil in place with a clip and apply a coating of white glue on one side. Make four coils in this way and, when the glue has set, position them on the binding around the pot and attach them with a glue gun.

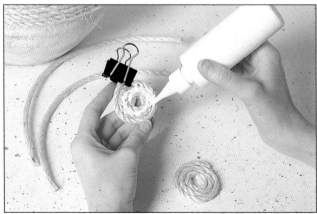

PROJECT 35

Valentine Box

YOU WILL NEED
a cardboard box
rope
scissors
white thread
glue

A true love knot makes a beautifully simple statement on Valentine's day or at any time. Here it is used to decorate a box, but it could be made into a hair clip or a buckle.

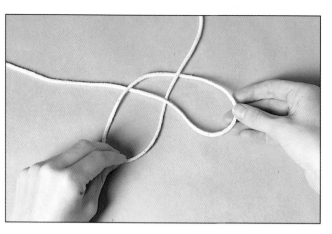

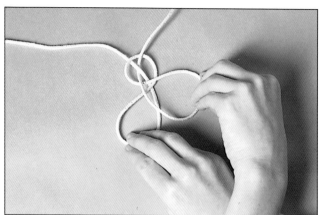

1 | *Measure and cut 7' of fine rope. Bend it in the middle and pass the left strand over to the right and pass the right strand through the loop and to the left. Open out the knot by pulling the two lower loops.*

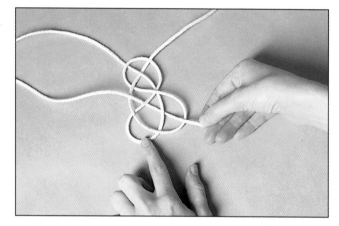

2 | *Hold the loops in place with your left hand. Pick up the strand at the top left and weave it through the knot as shown: over, under, under, over the other strands of the knot.*

3 | *Hold a loop in each hand and twist the loops once to the left, then cross the left hand over the right hand. Make sure the loose shape is roughly the size you require the finished knot to be.*

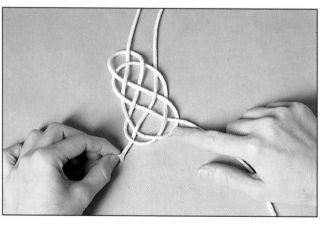

4 | *Pick up the strand at the top right and weave it as shown: under, over, under, over, under the other strands of the knot. Loop the two strands at the bottom to match that at the top. Take one strand and follow the path of the other strand to form a double knot. Repeat this with the other strand to form a triple love knot.*

5 | *When the two ends meet, secure the four strands in pairs with white thread as shown. Make sure this will not be visible from the other side. Trim the ends and glue the love knot onto the lid of a round box. Glue a rope trim around the lid and at the base of the box.*

PROJECT 36

Rope Tassel

YOU WILL NEED

thick sisal rope
gold thread
scissors
a wooden bead

Passementerie, the art of making tassels and other trimmings,
has come back into fashion in recent years. Here is a very
natural version of the craft, made with sisal rope.

1 Cut two pieces of thick sisal rope, each 4 " in length and separate the strands. Tie a long gold thread around the middle of one strand and loosen the sisal fibers.

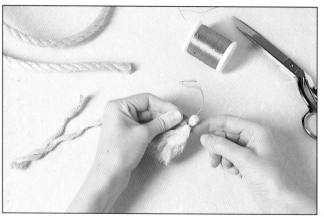

2 Bend the strand in the middle and bind another gold thread tightly around the top to form a tassel head. Knot the binding thread and trim the tassel ends neatly. Make six small tassels in this way.

3 Cut an 8 " piece of thick sisal rope and lay the hanging threads of the small tassels along it. Thread this combination through a wooden bead. Separate the strands of the rope on one side of the bead as shown.

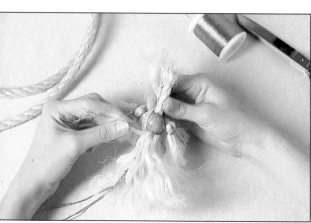

4 Turn the tassel upside down. Pull separate strands of sisal back over the bead, arranging the small tassels at intervals as you work. Bind the loose strands around rope with gold thread. Knot the hanging threads of the small tassels at the top to form a hanging loop.

Cane

Basketry is one of the oldest and most skilled of traditional crafts. People of different cultures developed different basketry methods according to the natural materials around them but, regardless of whether you are using cane, willow, honeysuckle, or other plant materials, many of the principles remain the same. In this chapter, cane is used to show some of these techniques.

Cane is harvested from the rattan creeper which grows to enormous lengths in southeast Asia. The outer layer of the vine is discarded. The pith core is milled into canes of varying thicknesses, ranging from #000 (thin) to #16 (thick). Cane can be bought in bundles from some craft shops or from specialist suppliers listed in the telephone directory. Cane is quite inexpensive and each bundle will contain enough for several projects so there is plenty of allowance for making early

mistakes. Cane can be dyed with vegetable or fabric dyes, although the natural straw color is very attractive unadorned.

To make the cane flexible enough for working, it must be soaked in water for about thirty minutes. If it dries while you are working, wrap a damp cloth around it or just re-soak it until it is manageable once more. When a project is finished, allow it and the remaining cane to dry completely, as damp cane can become moldy.

Household implements can be used for many projects. Strong scissors or secateurs are needed, as well as a bodkin, which is a sharp implement for piercing the cane and manipulating it: a metal knitting needle or a screwdriver can be substituted. Clothes pegs or bulldog clips are especially handy for holding your work temporarily in place while you give your hands a rest.

The first project in this chapter is very simple, but will give you a feel for working with cane. Projects 38 and 39 introduce you to the two main types of basketry: using a hard base and a woven base.

Grades of cane
Cane is milled to different thicknesses. From left to right: #3, #5 and #8. For complex projects, such as baskets, you will need various grades: thick cane for the base spokes or stakes and thinner ones for weaving. Extra thick grades are available for forming handles.

Wreath base
Cane twisted into a coil can then be used as a base for pretty dried or fresh flowers. Use a glue gun to secure the flowers and add moss or foliage to soften the outlines.

Basketry
Basketry can be worked by weaving upright canes through holes in a base board, or by weaving a base from canes which are then bent to form upright stakes. The steps for the tablemats in Project 39 replicate the start of a woven base basket.

PROJECT 37

Candle Ring

The flexibility of cane is put to good use in this simple candle ring, while a touch of gold paint brings out the rich hue of the beeswax candle.

YOU WILL NEED
cane (#5 or #8)
a basin
wire
gold paint
a brush
a thick candle
a gold pen

1 ▶ Soak several lengths of cane in a basin of water for ten minutes. Shape the end of one cane into a ring with a diameter 1 " larger than that of your candle. Secure the cane ring with a piece of wire.

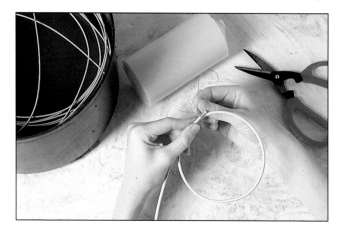

2 ◀ Holding the ring in one hand, thread the other end of the cane through and turn the ring, coiling it. Continue until you have a sturdy coil of cane. If necessary, add a new cane, holding the ends together until they are secured by later coils.

3 ▶ Apply a coat of gold paint to a length of cane, using a brush or spray paint. When the paint is touch dry, coil this piece around the ring as before. Secure the end by tucking it under a previous coil and then trim it neatly.

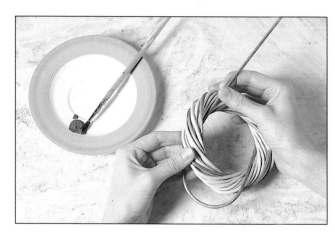

4 ▶ Check that the candle base will fit into the ring. Use a gold pen to draw stars on the candle.

NOTE: Never leave any candle burning unattended.

PROJECT 38

Breakfast Tray

Few things are nicer than breakfast in bed: one of them is breakfast in bed on a hand woven tray. This example of hard-base weaving is easier than it appears.

1 Measure and cut a 12 " x 16 " piece of plywood or other board, rounding the corners with a coping saw. Mark and drill 71 holes around the perimeter: use a drill bit large enough to accommodate your cane. Apply several coats of varnish to the base board.

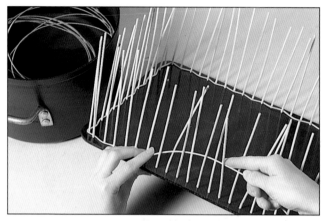

2 Cut 71 pieces of #5 cane, each 8 " long. Soak these "uprights" in water for fifteen minutes. Insert them in the holes and, on the under-side of the base, weave them as shown.

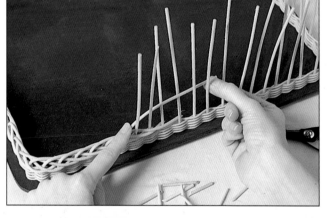

3 Soak several lengths of #3 cane for 10 minutes. Lay one end of a cane inside an upright and weave the length behind the next upright, then in front, and so on. Continue weaving in and out until you have circled the board nine times. Add in a new length by overlapping the old and new ends on the inside of an upright.

4 To weave the rim, the uprights must be made pliable again, so stand the tray upside down in a basin of water. Weave the rim by bending the first upright behind the next two, in front of the two after that, and finally behind the next. Trim the end neatly on the inside. You will need to loosen the beginning of the rim to insert the last few uprights.

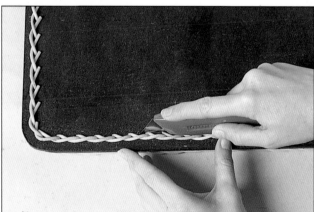

5 Neaten the underside of the tray by trimming the ends of the uprights at an angle with a sharp knife.

PROJECT 39

Table Mats

YOU WILL NEED
cane (#3, #5 & #8)
a basin
a knife
strong scissors
a ruler
a piercing tool

These sturdy cane mats are woven in the same way as the bases of many baskets. The simplest method of finishing the mat is by "whaling," inserting loops of cane.

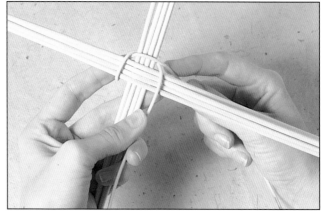

1 Cut eight stakes, each 10" long, from #8 cane. On four of these, shave one end into a point. Pierce the middle of the others with a sharp tool such as a bodkin or skewer. Push these stakes through the holes to form a "slath."

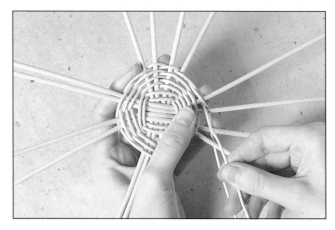

2 Soak several #3 canes in water for 10 minutes. Bend one in half and loop it around a slath arm. Take one end over the next arm and the other behind it, then bring the back one forward and take the front one back. Continue weaving like this until you've circled the slath twice.

3 With your fingers, divide the next arm into two pairs and weave between them. Work around the slath to form eight arms. Continue weaving in this way for another two rounds.

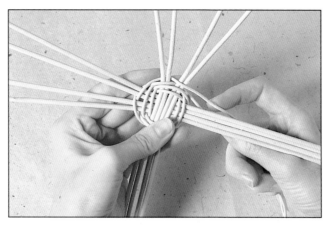

4 On the next round, divide all the pairs to form single spokes and weave between them. Continue weaving until the mat is 8½" in diameter. If you need to join in a new piece of cane, overlap the old and the new ends and trim to neaten. Secure the ends of the weavers by threading them through the previous round.

5 Cut and soak 16 pieces of #5 cane, each 5½" long. Point all ends. Insert the end of one alongside one of the stakes (make a gap first with a bodkin or knitting needle if necessary). Insert the other end of the cane alongside the next stake to form a loop. Insert all the stakes in this way.

Clay

Making a useful or decorative object from a formless lump of material is a very satisfying pastime. Moreover, the sensation of molding and working clay is especially enjoyable and therapeutic, if a little messy at times.

Natural clay contains many tiny plate-shaped particles and some water. If there is sufficient water, the flat particles can slide around, making it possible to shape the clay. When the water is reduced, the clay becomes stiff and brittle. Once dry, natural clay can be hardened by firing it in a kiln or even in a bonfire. However, clay compounds which harden by being exposed to air are now available. This self-hardening clay is relatively expensive and containers made will not hold water, but it is a good alternative for simple projects. Some of these clays can also be fired in a kiln, if you have access to one.

Expensive equipment is not essential: you do not need a potter's wheel to create interesting pieces. You will need a piece of wire for cutting slabs, a rolling pin, and various household objects for shaping, cutting, and marking the clay.

To create tiles or flat slabs of even thickness, roll the clay between two matching pieces of wood until the rolling pin rests on the wood at either side. Long rolls of clay are useful in many projects such as cylindrical beads and pots formed with a long coil. Roll them roughly by hand and then use a tile or another flat object to roll them evenly.

Mark patterns in clay using improvised stamps: a small tree cone, star anise, and shells would all leave interesting impressions. Textures can also be impressed with materials such as netting or with a wire brush or a rasp.

Acrylic paints and colored gouache give a strong opaque covering on clay. Apply a coat of varnish afterward to protect the piece and to strengthen the colors.

Start with small projects such as buttons and beads. Tiles offer an excellent opportunity to experiment with textures and colors and make interesting gifts as teapot stands, nameplates, or as commemorative plaques to celebrate a wedding or birth.

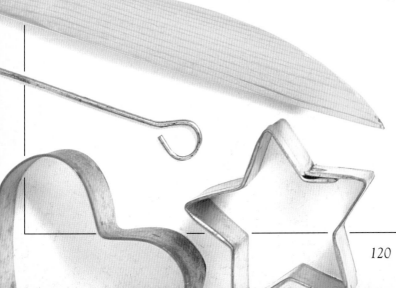

Special tools can be purchased for shaping clay, but household items make good substitutes.

To prepare clay for shaping and modeling, expel any air bubbles by slamming it down onto the work surface until it becomes easy to shape. Keep excess clay well packaged while not in use, or it will dry out.

Sample projects
The fish motif has been modeled in relief and marked with a knife. Some beads have been pierced with a skewer and patterned with wire.

Breadwarmer
Heated clay tiles can be added to a basket of oven-fresh bread to keep it warm. Traditionally, such tiles were decorated with sheaves of wheat and other harvest symbols.

PROJECT 40

String of Beads

YOU WILL NEED
air-drying clay
black paint
gold paint
toothpick
paint brushes
nylon thread
a necklace clasp

Stylish beads are all the more special if you make them yourself. You only need a small amount of clay and some paint to create beads of all shapes and forms.

1 ▶ Break off a lump of clay and roll it into a long sausage. Slice it into even segments and then roll each one between the palms of your hands to form balls. Roll a thinner sausage and slice it neatly into even segments to form long beads. Pierce a hole in each bead with a toothpick.

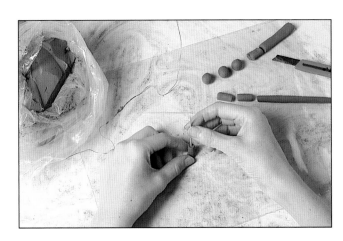

2 ▶ Pick up each bead on the point of a thick toothpick or some other object which holds it securely. Apply a coat of black acrylic paint and allow it to dry before applying a second coat. A piece of polystyrene can hold the toothpicks while the beads are drying.

3 ▶ With a fine brush, paint golds stripes on the cylindrical beads and gold spirals on the round beads. When the gold paint is dry, apply a coat of gloss varnish.

4 ▶ Thread the beads onto a double length of wire or nylon thread. Check the length of the necklace before tying a large knot in each end. Attach the sections of a clasp at either end.

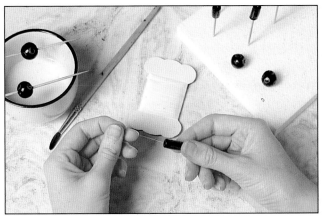

PROJECT 41

Windchimes

The sun and stars make up this delightful mobile which will twirl in a breeze. If you also want a pleasant tinkling sound, you will need to fire the pieces in a kiln.

1 ▶ *Roll out a slab of clay to a thickness of ¼ ". Cut a disk 4 " in diameter to form the hanging plate. Cut another disk 2½ " in diameter: this is the chime. Using a skewer, pierce a center hole in each disk and pierce five holes around the hanging plate, ½ " in from the edge.*

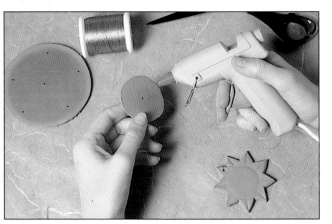

2 ◀ *Cut card templates from the patterns. Use these to cut thirteen stars and one sun from the clay. Press the skewer into the rays of each shape as shown. Pierce a single hole in the top of the sun and in five of the stars. In the remaining stars, pierce a hole at the top and another at the bottom.*

3 ◀ *Once the clay pieces have dried, cut an 8 " piece of strong thread and tie the sun onto one end. Thread the other end through the chime and secure it halfway with a dab of glue. Tie the stars in five chains of two or three, each with a single-hole star at the bottom.*

4 ◀ *Thread the chime–sun strand through the center of the hanging plate, tie a knot and secure it with a dab of glue. Thread the star chains through the perimeter holes, knotting them above and below the hanging plate and securing with dabs of glue. Gather the strands in a bunch above the plate and knot these together to form a loop.*

PROJECT 42

Festive Jigsaw

The dove, a symbol of peace, is a fitting image for a holiday jigsaw. This one, formed from clay, should be treated with some care.

YOU WILL NEED
air-drying clay
a rolling pin
pencils
tracing paper
a sharp knife
acrylic paints
acrylic varnish
a brush
a box

Mix 2 cups flour, 1 cup salt and ½ cup water together. Knead the mixture with your hands, gradually adding extra water

To tint the dough a single color, add food coloring to the water before you make the dough, or knead it in once the dough is made. Create a marbled effect by twisting together two sausages of differently colored dough and kneading them lightly.

4-9-2014

Notation
Two Pages Missing
from 126 to 130
Please in form library
of these finding
Carolyn Hill

Here, watercolors are applied directly onto the baked dough. The heart shapes on the right, cut with a cookie cutter with paperclip sections inserted as hanging loops, have been painted with an undercoat of white gesso and then with acrylic colors.

Sample projects
The unpainted wreath on the left was made by braiding three strands of dough and adding shaped leaves. The animals were cut using paper templates and then painted with acrylics.

PROJECT 43

Gilded Bowl

These bright and unusual dishes will strike a festive note at Christmas time. After use, wipe them clean with a damp cloth.

YOU WILL NEED

salt dough (see p128)
a baking dish
vegetable oil
a rolling pin & board
a sharp knife
a brush
gesso
acrylic paints
clear varnish

1 Make one quantity of salt dough, following the instructions on page 129. On a floured surface, roll out the dough to a thickness of ¼". Select a heatproof dish with a rim and grease the dish lightly with vegetable oil.

2 Lay the rolled dough in the dish and gently ease it into shape. Trim the edge with a sharp knife, forming a rim. Cut triangle shapes from the excess dough and smooth the edges of these with a moistened finger.

3 Moisten the back of each triangle and press them onto the rim of the dough bowl. Add a circle of triangles in the center of the dish. Bake the dish in a low oven (250°F) for 4 hours, piercing any air bubbles which form. Remove the heatproof dish and continue to bake the dough dish for another 4 hours.

4 When the dish has cooled, coat the entire piece in gesso. Apply several coats of acrylic paint to the whole piece. When it is dry, paint each triangle gold. Apply several coats of acrylic varnish, leaving the pieces to dry between each coat.

PROJECT 44

Magnets

Magnets are especially popular with children who will adore these cheerful fish shapes. The young at heart can also use them to hold notes on the refrigerator or filing cabinet.

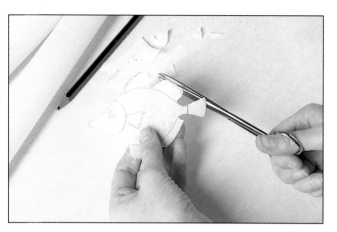

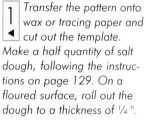

1 Transfer the pattern onto wax or tracing paper and cut out the template. Make a half quantity of salt dough, following the instructions on page 129. On a floured surface, roll out the dough to a thickness of ¼ ".

2 Lay the template on the dough and carefully cut around it with a sharp knife. Cut out all the fish you require. From the offcuts, shape an extra fin for each fish. Smooth all the edges with a moistened finger.

3 Mark the eyes, scales, and fins with the tip of the knife or with a large needle. Moisten the back of the extra fin and press it onto the fish body. Put the fish on a baking dish and bake for an hour in the oven at 250°F. Remove the pieces from the oven and leave them to cool.

4 Mix watercolor paints on a dish and apply them delicately to the fish with a fine brush. Allow the paint to dry. Apply several coats of clear varnish, leaving the pieces to dry between each coat. Secure a small magnet to the back of each fish with strong glue.

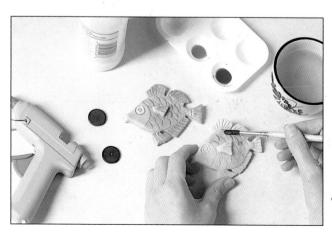

PROJECT 45

Wall Plaque

Baskets of fruit and sheaves of wheat are traditional subjects for dough artists. This design, which combines various shaping techniques, celebrates the harvest.

1 ▶ Make one quantity of salt dough, following the instructions on page 129. Cut an oval-shape piece of wax paper. On a floured surface, roll out the dough to a thickness of ¼ ". Lay the oval template on the dough and carefully cut around it with a sharp knife. Cut a hole in the top third to form a hanging loop.

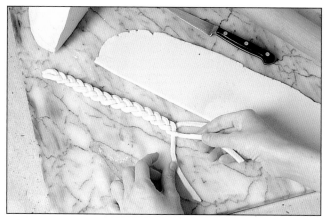

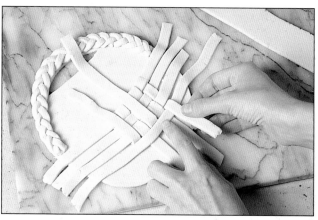

2 ▲ Cut three long strips of dough and smooth the edges. Braid them in a three-strand braid (see page 13). Brush water around the rim of the top half of the oval and position the braid to form the basket handle. Carefully trim the ends of the braid.

3 ▲ Cut more long strips of dough and lay one strip across the oval in a slight curve. Lay the next strip at a right angle to the first. Keep laying dough strips at right angles to each other, weaving them over and under to form a lattice. Trim the ends to fit the oval and secure them with dabs of water.

4 ▶ Cut fruit shapes from the remaining dough and mold them with your fingers. Check that each piece will fit in the available area, then moisten the back and press it into place. Mark the leaf veins, strawberry seeds, and pineapple sections. Insert cloves as stalks.

5 ▶ Transfer the basket to a baking dish and bake it for 12 hours in the oven at 250°F. When the piece has cooled, apply several coats of clear varnish, allowing the varnish to dry between coats.

Wax

Wax comes in a range of forms: it is essentially a solid substance which has a low melting point. This makes it suitable as a burning fuel for producing light. Wax from berries and plants was one of the earliest sources of light, used in prehistoric times. Later, when the majority of candles were made from tallow, animal fat which produced much smoke and smell, beeswax candles were used by those who could afford them. Paraffin wax, a by-product of petroleum oil, was found to be suitable for candlemaking in the nineteenth century, and this is still the most commonly used wax.

Paraffin wax can be bought in solid blocks or in granular form. The simplest of all candles to make is a glassful of these wax granules, with a wick in the center and perhaps a little scent added. Melted wax can be poured into containers such as large shells or small pots, as in Project 46, or into a mold. Freestanding molded candles burn better than those in containers.

Beeswax is available in blocks or in preformed sheets. The latter can simply be rolled around a wick as shown on the next page. Beeswax candles burn more slowly than paraffin ones and give off a delicious scent of warm honey.

Candle wicks, braided and treated strings bought from craft shops, come in different thicknesses. They are named according to the thickness of candle that they suit: a 1 " wick burns a 1 " candle. Molds can be bought or improvised using any container which will hold hot wax and from which the finished candle can be easily removed. Wax, like cooking oil, will catch fire if overheated. If wax you are melting starts to smoke, turn the heat off. If it catches fire, smother it with the lid of the saucepan.

There are, of course, many other craft uses for wax. Among its other properties, it is waterproof, making it a natural protective barrier for the skin when used in moisturizers and other cosmetics. It can also be used for resist painting: draw a pattern with pure wax or with wax crayons and cover it with a wash of watercolor for a lovely effect.

Dipping candles
One traditional method of making candles is to dip a wick into melted wax repeatedly, allowing time for it to harden slightly between dippings.

To roll a beeswax candle, lay a wick along a side edge. Trim the top edge at an angle for a candle with a cone-shaped top. Fold the side edge tightly over the wick. Pinch a small piece of wax from the base and reserve it. Roll the candle and press the edge down firmly. Pinch reserved wax around the wick to prime it.

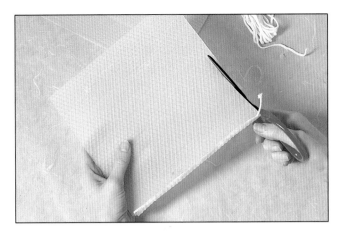

1 Dip a wick in a little melted wax. When cool, tie one end around a skewer. Lay this over the opening of the mold. Thread the wick through a hole in the base of the mold and secure it with modeling clay. Melt wax in a bowl over simmering water. If using paraffin wax, add 1 part of stearin, a hardening agent, to every 9 parts wax.

2 Pour the melted mixture slowly into the mold. Tap it gently to release air bubbles. After an hour, a depression will have formed around the wick. Break the skin and top it up with more melted wax. When the candle is cool, remove it by tapping the mold. Smooth the base by holding the candle over a heated saucepan.

Decorating candles
Arrange pressed flowers around the lower section of a candle and brush on melted wax to secure them in place. Do not leave decorated candles burning unattended as the flowers may ignite.

PROJECT 46

Candle Pots

YOU WILL NEED
paraffin wax
wax crayons
wicks
essential oil
terracotta pots
adhesive clay
skewers
a bowl
a saucepan

These simple flower-pot candles are a delightful addition to a table. They are extremely easy to make, and will add color and perfume to any occasion.

1 ▶ Melt some paraffin wax in a bowl over a saucepan of water. Select wick thread of a suitable thickness. Measure a length of wick slightly higher than your pot, coat it with wax, and pull it straight. When it is cool, tie one end around a skewer to form a wick rod.

2 ▶ Make sure the terracotta pot is clean. Lay the wick rod across the top of the pot and thread the loose end through the drainage hole. Plug the hole with adhesive clay or plasticine. If your pot has no drainage hole, secure the wick end to the base with a piece of adhesive clay.

3 ▶ Add more paraffin wax to the bowl and melt it slowly over simmering water. Do not leave the wax unattended. Add shavings of wax crayon for coloring and a few drops of essential oil to scent the candle.

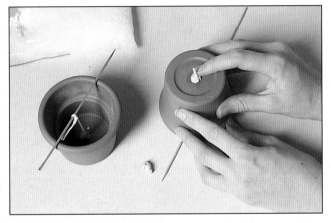

4 ▶ Slowly pour the melted wax into the pot until it is three-quarters full. Tap the sides gently to release any air bubbles. After an hour, a depression will have formed around the wick. Break the skin with a skewer and top it up with more melted wax. Leave the candle to cool and then trim the wick.

PROJECT 47

Hand Cream

Beeswax offers a natural protection for the skin. This recipe is especially soothing for dry hands and makes a lovely gift when presented in a pretty jar.

1 ▶ Measure out 1 oz of beeswax and 1 oz of glycerin. Melt them together in a bowl over a saucepan of simmering water or in a double boiler.

2 ▶ When the wax and the glycerin are completely liquid, stir in 1½ fl oz of rose water as well as 2½ fl oz of almond oil.

3 ▶ Remove the saucepan from the heat and leave the bowl standing in the hot water. Add 1 teaspoonful of honey, 5 drops of rose oil, and 10 drops of lemon juice, and stir vigorously until the mixture is blended.

4 ◀ Pour the mixture into a ceramic bowl and beat it continuously as it cools: an electric beater may be required to get a smooth consistency. Store the cream in a screw-top jar and label it with a name and the date. If it is a gift, cut a circle of fabric and tie it over the lid.

PROJECT 48

Batik Giftwrap

This bright paper is decorated with Os and Xs carrying a message of love. The project, a good introduction to the art of batik, requires only household items.

1 Select large sheets of white paper which do not have a glossy coating. Dissolve 1 teaspoon baking soda (sodium bicarbonate) and 1 teaspoon washing soda (sodium carbonate) in 3 cups warm water. Sponge the paper with the soda solution and leave the soaked paper to dry.

2 Cut two strips of cardboard, cut a slot lengthwise in each and fix them together to form a cross. Cut a section of strong cardboard tubing. These shapes are called "caps" in batik work.

3 Lay a sheet of the soda-treated paper on a folded towel. Melt paraffin wax or beeswax (or a combination of the two) in a bowl over boiling water. Dip the end of a cap into the wax and press it onto the paper. The wax should soak in and discolor the paper. Mark alternating rows of Os and Xs.

4 Dip a sponge in strong food coloring or a fabric dye and wipe a series of diagonal lines over the paper (you might want to protect your hands with rubber gloves). Fill in the gaps with lines of a contrasting color and leave the paper to dry.

5 Place the decorated paper between sheets of scrap paper and press with a warm iron. The wax will seep out, leaving white Os and Xs on your giftwrap.

Wood

Wood is a fascinating material for anyone interested in craftwork. From supple twigs to seasoned timber, there is such variety of colors, textures, and other properties that wood offers almost unlimited possibilities. Some pieces—weathered driftwood or a twisted twig—can be incorporated in projects as they are found. Others beg for special treatment such as shaping, fixing, or a decorative finish.

In spring, many trees shoot out long twigs which are very flexible and can be twisted into wreath bases or baskets without breaking. Willow, hickory, hazel, laurel, and rhododendron are all ideal for this purpose. To shape a wreath base from twigs or vines, first cross over the ends and pull them to form a circle in the middle. Wrap one end around this circle in a long spiral, then wrap the other end in the opposite direction and secure both ends by tucking them under an earlier round. Extra lengths can be woven in to make the base thicker.

Fall or winter twigs which have lost their suppleness still have much to offer.

Straight twigs can be cut into short or long sections, drilled, and used as beads or pencils. Project 49 offers another possibility. Twigs can also be glued to decorate frames or to make planters for small terracotta pots.

Timber can and should be recycled. Old fence palings and floor boards can be turned into works of art with an unusual paint finish. Wood can be stained with natural dyes, or painted and then distressed to reveal the natural grain.

Soft woods can be carved without an array of expensive and specialized tools. Balsa wood can even be shaped with a potato peeler or a craft knife. Pine can be carved roughly with a coping saw and then shaped further with a strong knife. Choose simple projects to begin with: a decoy duck or a toy, where primitive lines are part of the article's appeal.

Plywood can be cut with a coping saw to create plaques, weathervanes, and other flat articles in the shapes of angels, hands, and other designs. Smooth the edges with sandpaper and paint details in bold colors. Small stars, suns, and hearts can be drilled and hung in a window or on the Christmas tree.

Sections of branches make rustic coasters. Bark and the shavings created when working with a plane can also be used as craft materials.

Dominoes
Saw a length of timber into short, even sections. Heat a skewer over a gas flame or on an electric element and brand a line across each piece. Twist the end of a length of wire to form a circle. Heat this as above and brand the appropriate number of dots on each domino. Pyrography should be worked with great care.

Candle wraps
Sticks of cinnamon can be used as a substitute for twigs in projects such as this candle holder. Do not leave any candles burning unattended.

Twig pencils
Cut a fresh twig from a tree. Bend a coathanger wire at a right angle and twist one end of this "drill" into the pulp center. Remove the wire regularly and shake out scraps of pulp. Roll a graphite rod in glue and push it into the hole. When the glue is dry, sharpen the pencil with a knife.

Wreath base
These fine twigs have simply been coiled and bound into a small circle with another supple twig.

PROJECT 49

Napkin Rings

These twiggy napkin rings are ideal if you want to strike an informal note at a special meal. Wrap a short candle in the same way and add it to the festive table.

YOU WILL NEED
a cardboard tube
straight twigs
a ruler & pencil
a knife & mat
a small handsaw
a glue gun
scissors
raffia

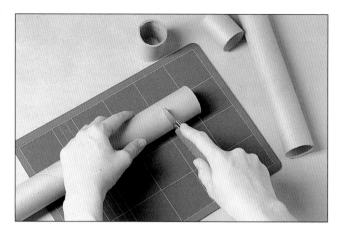

1 Measure 2" from the end of a strong cardboard tube and mark a pencil line around it. Cut along the line with a sharp knife. Cut as many rings as you require.

2 Select twigs that are reasonably straight and cut them into 3" lengths with a small saw. You will need quite a few twig sections to surround the cardboard ring: test whether you have enough by holding them in place temporarily with an elastic band.

3 Holding the cardboard ring in one hand, apply glue from a hot glue gun onto the middle of the tubing and place a twig section onto the glue. Work around the ring, gluing several twigs on each time and making sure that they fit neatly together.

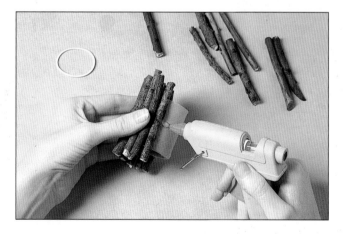

4 Decorate the napkin ring with a binding of raffia, tied in a knot or a bow. Make different rings with varying shades of twigs for a varied effect.

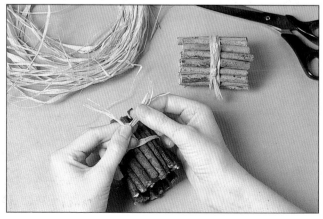

PROJECT 50

Mirror Frame

Recycled timber from an old fence or shed can be given a second life with an interesting paint treatment and a few natural decorations.

YOU WILL NEED
old timber palings
a handsaw
a tape measure
a hammer & nails
wood wash
a sponge
wet-&-dry paper
a glue gun
a mirror
decorative objects

1 ◄ Measure and cut a series of timber pieces for the back panel and glue these together. Measure and cut the frame sections, cutting the ends at a right angle so they fit together. Glue these mitered edges together. Secure the frame onto the back panel with nails through the back.

2 ◄ Stir the wood wash well. Apply a coat with a brush and within a few minutes wipe the painted surface with a damp sponge. Leave the frame to dry as per the instructions on the label.

3 ► To reveal more of the grain and give the frame a worn appearance, rub the paint-work lightly with a wet piece of wet-&-dry paper. This is especially useful if you have had to use a paint other than wood wash. If the mirror is to be used in a bathroom or other damp place, apply one or more coats of varnish.

4 ► Ask a glazier to cut a mirror to size. Glue the mirror into the frame. Arrange a few shells, starfish, or other natural objects around the corners and glue them in place with a glue gun. Attach a hook or wire to the back if the mirror is to be hung on a wall.

PROJECT 51

Collector's Box

YOU WILL NEED
plywood
timber
a handsaw
sandpaper
panel pins
a hammer
white glue
a tape measure
a pencil
an eraser

This display box is a modern version of the old printer's tray, used to hold metal type. It is an attractive way to show off nature's diversity and to remember places you have been.

1 Measure and cut a 10" square of plywood. Measure and cut the following pieces of ¼" timber: 2 x 10", 4 x 9½", 5 x 3". Sand any rough edges smooth.

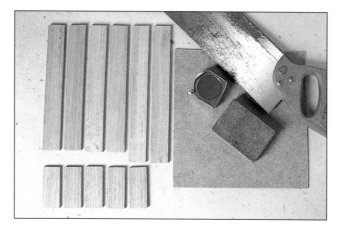

2 Glue the two long pieces and two of the medium pieces to form a frame. Secure this with two panel pins at each corner. Glue the frame to the base board and secure it by hammering panel pins through the base and into the frame.

3 Measure and mark the position for the two center strips. Glue them in place and then secure them with two panel pins hammered in at either end.

4 Measure and mark the positions for the five small strips. Make sure they fit neatly: you may need to sand the edges further or even to cut fresh pieces. Glue them in place. Erase all pencil marks. When the glue is set, fill the sections with seeds, shells and other natural items, balancing colors and shapes to please the eye.

Gift Giving

Everyone knows the enjoyment of giving something special to someone dear to you. The other side of the coin is the pleasure of receiving something that someone has made especially for you. It need not be elaborate, but the fact that the giver has spent some time and thought making it is far more valuable than any price tag another gift might have carried.

This book is filled with projects which make wonderful gifts and which can be adapted slightly and made into unique presents. Think about friends' preferred colors or their favorite scents and choose ribbons or essential oils accordingly.

Make gifts that will fit into people's homes: if they like the country style, add lots of raffia; if their decorating scheme is more formal, use a sophisticated wired ribbon.

Think about the way you package and present your gift. Pages 154–5 give a few ideas for using natural resources to wrap and decorate a gift. Pages 156–7 offer suggestions for making greeting cards and gift tags embellished with flowers and other materials.

In these pressured times when technology changes before we even get a chance to understand it, a little bit of timeless nature is possibly the best gift you can offer someone.

Pure ornament
Unusual and attractive pieces of jewelry can be fashioned from nuts, shells, seeds, and feathers to suit individuals with a taste for decoration. See Projects 12, 17, and 40 for some ideas to get you started.

Natural cosmetics
For those who care for healthy skin and prefer a natural alternative to commercial products, homemade cosmetics make a wonderful gift. Projects 22 and 47 offer a few ways to use natural ingredients for skincare.

Nature's harvest
Everyone appreciates edible treats such as jams and preserves. A box of bouquet garnis or a bottle of herb vinegar make thoughtful gifts for a keen cook. See Projects 4, 9, and 23 for some suggestions.

Wrapping Gifts

Nature is the ultimate designer and you need look no further for gift wrapping ideas. Forget the expensive and unremarkable rolls of garish paper for sale; stroll through the garden or raid the pantry and you'll find plenty of raw materials for great presentation.

For a very natural effect, use plain brown paper and embellish it with twine or raffia and small sprays of berries or spice bundles. Corrugated card has a delightful texture and wraps well around bottles or jars. Fabrics such as hessian and calico also make interesting wrapping materials.

All these materials can be decorated with paint if you want a little color on your gift-wrap. Cut motifs in a halved potato or use a leaf or a halved orange to print repeat patterns in bright colors. A few stars and suns can turn a humble brown paper bag into a charming gift bag.

In place of curling ribbon, use webbing, sisal rope, or paper ribbon as trimmings. Natural gift tags can be made by securing large leaves and writing your message with gold pen.

At Christmas time, a touch of gold adds a sense of occasion. Spray brown paper lightly with gold paint and trim parcels with gold-sprayed leaves and seedpods.

Giftwrap
Orange prints adorn the sweet cone; green paint has been sprayed with a toothbrush over fern leaves to cover the box.

Packaging
Petals, either fresh or dried, make delightful packaging for delicate gifts. Wood shavings, scented with a few drops of essential oil, are a good alternative.

Making Tags & Cards

Card crafting is one of the best ways to develop new skills and produce results quickly. Handmade cards are always superior to the bought kind, especially when made with handmade paper (see pages 14–15).

Shells, flowers, stars, and other natural forms are easy to represent in simplified designs and make ideal motifs for potato-prints or stenciling. The cream-colored card below has been impressed with grains of rice and some string arranged to look like wheat.

Most greeting cards are single folds with a design on the front. To frame a design in a card, use a three-panel mount such as the one on the bottom right of page 157. Blank mounts can be bought in craft shops or you can make your own by folding a piece of card into three panels and cutting a window in the center panel.

If a card will be put in an envelope and so needs to be flat, you could decorate it with pressed plant materials. Gift tags, on the other hand, can be adorned with small seeds, berries, or whatever you choose. Tags can be cut in any shape to suit the occasion or to suit the gift (if you like giving hints).

Photograms
The delicate and detailed shapes of many plants make them ideal subjects for this treatment. Objects are laid on a piece of photographic paper and exposed briefly to a light source from above. The paper is then processed as a black-and-white print would be: the area hit by light turns black while the rest remains white, giving a sharp silhouette.

From left to right:
A leaf print; a gift tag decorated with star anise; handmade paper impressed with a block; a ring of pressed larkspurs in a three-panel mount.

157

Celebrating the Seasons

All around the world, people have ritually celebrated the changing seasons with festivals of some kind. The early Christian church quickly recognized the strength of the pagan festive calendar and hitched religious events to it wherever possible.

Easter was originally an Anglo-Saxon spring festival which celebrated the time of rebirth and creation in the natural cycle, themes which fitted well with Christ's resurrection. The Jewish passover, held at the same time of the year, also celebrates a new lease of life. The decoration of eggs, symbols of this concept, is a widespread tradition. On the European continent, budding branches are also adorned as Easter trees.

Garlands of flowers are traditionally worn to mark mid-summer in some countries, while fall, a vitally important time of year for harvesting crops and preserving food, is still celebrated with harvest festivals in rural areas. The white settlers in America marked the success of their first harvest with Thanksgiving, a time when nature is given its due.

Halloween was once a pagan celebration to mark the end of the year according to the old Celtic calendar. It retains its un-Christian association with ghosts and goblins and offers a chance to make wonderful lanterns from hollowed pumpkins or squash.

Christmas is, for much of the world, a winter festivity and so is enjoyed amid swags of evergreens. The tradition of kissing under the mistletoe comes to us from centuries past, while the decoration of Christmas trees is a relatively recent custom from Germany. Yuletide, the precursor to Christmas, marked the shortest days of the year. It is growing as a mid-winter celebration for southern hemisphere countries such as Australia.

These earliest traditions, like the festivals of many other cultures, confirm our reliance on the natural world and the sustenance it affords us.

Spring
Flowers and eggs sum up spring nicely. Make a "nest" for painted eggs with loosely wound fibers and place it beside an arrangement of spring flowers.